THE LIVING
UNKNOWN
SOLDIER

THE LIVING UNKNOWN SOLDIER

A Story of Grief and the Great War

JEAN-YVES LE NAOUR

TRANSLATED BY PENNY ALLEN

METROPOLITAN BOOKS

Henry Holt and Company | New York

Metropolitan Books
Henry Holt and Company, LLC
Publishers since 1866
115 West 18th Street
New York, New York 10011

Metropolitan Books™ is a registered
trademark of Henry Holt and Company, LLC.

Distributed in Canada by H. B. Fenn and Company Ltd.

Originally published in France in 2002 under the title
Le Soldat Inconnu Vivant by Hachette Littératures

Library of Congress Cataloging-in-Publication Data

Le Naour, Jean-Yves.
    [Soldat inconnu vivant. English]
    The living unknown soldier : a story of grief and the Great War / by Jean-Yves Le
Naour ; translated by Penny Allen.—1st American ed.
        p. cm.
    ISBN 0-8050-7522-4
    1. Mangin, Anthelme, d. 1942.   2. Soldiers—France—Biography.   3. World War,
1914–1918—Unknown military personnel, French.   4. Amnesia—Patients—France.
    I. Title.
DC373.M2356L413 2004
940.4'1244'092—dc22
                                                                                            2004040276
[B]

Henry Holt books are available for special
promotions and premiums. For details contact:
Director, Special Markets.

First American Edition 2004

Designed by Paula Russell Szafranski

Printed in the United States of America

1 3 5 7 9 10 8 6 4 2

Introduction

"May I be pardoned, as I begin this account, for any past suffering I revive, any false hopes I awaken? It is the most touching, the cruelest story of the war that I tell, a story of the purest and most brutal symbolism."[1] With these words, Paul Bringuier, writing in the national evening newspaper *L'Intransigeant* in 1935, inaugurated a series of ten articles on the amnesiac soldier Anthelme Mangin. According to him, the man the newspapers called the "living unknown soldier" had been discovered wandering the platforms of the Lyon-Brotteaux railway station on February 1, 1918, after a convoy of returning prisoners had passed through. From that day on he lived in asylums for the insane, moving from Bron, a suburb of Lyon, to Clermont-Ferrand, then to Rodez—where he was kept for more than sixteen years—and finally to the Sainte-Anne hospital in Paris, where he died on September 10, 1942, without ever having recovered his memory. Some called him the only truly free man, as he was without past, without memory, without hatred, without identity or family. More often, though, he was called the last vestige, the last prisoner of the Great War.

In February 1922, in an effort to solve the problem of identifying a brutally traumatized soldier who was called Anthelme Mangin only because he had to have *some* name, the Ministry of Pensions had his photograph published in all the major national and regional newspapers. At the same time, veterans' organizations showed deference to their comrade by creating a poster to display in city halls throughout France. Within a few weeks, dozens of citizens had claimed to recognize the Rodez amnesiac as a son, a husband, or a brother missing in action but never officially declared dead. Nearly three hundred people asked for more information, and while most of them recognized their error as soon as they saw a better photograph or met with him in the Aveyron regional asylum, twenty families would press their claims in court. The litigation continued, with interminable expert testimony, until the unknown man's death.

What might sound like a simple news item was in fact much more. From 1914 to 1918, more than 250,000 soldiers vanished, leaving no trace beyond the notice of their disappearance in action. Their families, as a result, were plunged into silence and deprived of the certainty and closure that a body provides. After the armistice and the repatriation of prisoners, among whom these families hoped to find their missing relatives—perhaps they had been held secretly in German prisons—the most rational resolved to accept the deaths. But the appearance of Anthelme Mangin, this unbelievable resurrection of a vanished soldier, revived hope, and it came to embody the misery of all those who refused to mourn. Mangin was thus a symbol: in his anonymity and his madman's remove from the world of the living, he was like a twin to the Unknown Soldier buried beneath the Arc de Triomphe. He stood for both the suffering of the families of the missing, who sought to identify him as their own, and for France's difficulty in coming to terms with grief between the two world wars. He also became part of the literary myth of the return of the soldier—a myth whose wide currency after 1918 suggested how guilty the living felt toward the conflict's dead. It was hardly surprising that Jean Anouilh should use Anthelme Mangin to create the hero of his *Traveler without Luggage,* first staged in 1937—at the very moment the lunatic was surrounded by experts who were trying to decide among the litigating families.

Mangin fascinated his contemporaries, who reported the details of his plight in the columns of the largest newspapers. However, revisiting his story has been fraught with pitfalls, because there is no record of his case in law archives, except for the minutes from rulings by the Rodez court and the Montpellier court of appeals. Documents and reports kept by the claims division of the Ministry of Pensions were destroyed in June 1940, before the arrival of German troops. Fortunately, in the Aveyron regional archives there is still a large file of correspondence between the Rodez asylum administration, the Aveyron prefect, and various families, and most of my information was drawn from this source.[2] The truth, though, is that Mangin really had no story of his own.

His story was in the suffering of the families who claimed him—which is why I have neither simply retraced his history nor written a classical biography here. Rather, I have attempted to set up some frontiers or borders for historians, and to understand the sadness of mourning, in its privacy and madness.

Chapter One

The Soldier without an Armistice

(1918–1922)

Bringuier's report of a mysterious soldier wandering the plat-forms of the Lyon-Brotteaux station gave rise to many more news items, sometimes contradictory and often romanticized. It was clear the soldier had been shipped from Germany in a convoy of disabled and severely wounded prisoners, proba-bly on a train that left Konstanz on January 30, 1918, head-ing for Lyon via Switzerland. From there, the stories diverged. In some, "Anthelme Mangin" either got off in Lyon on his own initiative or was separated from his companions when they were dispatched to various hospitals. Others theorized that the German authorities had simply jettisoned the amne-siac on the first available train without providing any papers for him. The *Courrier de l'Aveyron* fumed, "One might rea-sonably ask how it is that the German administration, which considers itself so perfect, returned sick men to us without even having the decency to tell us who they are. But we've seen it all before!"[1]

Nothing in particular distinguished the "poor vet."[2] He had no identity papers, he had lost his dog tag, and the number of his regiment had long since fallen off his threadbare overcoat. A search through his pockets turned up only a cigarette lighter made from a Mauser cartridge,[3] and just about every soldier possessed this kind of thing.

In one of a series of articles titled "The Enigma of the Living Unknown Soldier," published from May 11 to May 20, 1935 in *L'Intransigeant*, Paul Bringuier referred to February 1, 1918, as the day that marked the birth of Anthelme Mangin. Other newspapers took up his report, which was larded with mistakes, including passages where, for lack of real information, Bringuier gave free rein to his imagination. He conjured up icy rain, night, and fog to lend a gloomy ambience to the scene of the amnesiac's discovery by a military policeman, lantern in hand on his rounds, who finds him prostrate next to an iron pillar, shivering with cold and fever:[4]

> "Hey! What are you doing there?"
>
> "I don't know."
>
> "Were you on the train from Constance?"
>
> "I don't know."
>
> The policeman raises his lantern. He sees a waxen face with two weeks' beard and a blank stare. The man is wearing a dirty old infantryman's overcoat without insignia, a filthy cap, corduroy civilian trousers, and galoshes.

"What's your name?"
"I don't know."

At police headquarters, the interrogation continues. He is shaken, cursed, accused of faking, and threatened with court-martial. He remains silent, but in his exhaustion he finally blurts out "Mangin."

"What's that? Mangin? . . . Is that your name?"
"No."
"So why did you say 'Mangin'?"
"I don't know."

The military authorities soon enough realize that it is pointless to continue questioning the unknown man. He is sent to the psychiatric asylum in Bron and interned there as No. 13.[5]

Apart from this final fact—the only verified one in the account—these events existed solely in the mind of a journalist with a vivid imagination. In addition to a document denying the existence of any wandering soldier, which was made public only in 1937, several aspects of the account cast doubt on its veracity. First of all, the unknown man did not arrive in Lyon on some convoy or other, but specifically as one of sixty-five shell-shocked or demented repatriates.[6] Further, when Le Petit Parisien, a national morning newspaper, published photographs of six amnesiac soldiers[7] on January 10, 1920, three of them were still hospitalized in the Bron asylum. One Berrinet, interned there since February 1, 1918, had probably been on the same convoy as Anthelme Mangin, who had been sent to the asylum in Clermont-Ferrand on the day of the photographs' publication. Given Mangin's condition, it is especially difficult to believe the gendarmes could have for an instant suspected him of desertion or fraud, and it is even more difficult to imagine, with Bringuier, that such a suspicion could have persisted in the asylum, since the prisoners repatriated from Germany were anything but sound—that was precisely why the enemy had gotten rid of them. Once in France, their treatment was what came to be known as "the gentle cure," developed by a specialist named Damaye:[8] hot baths, regular meals, plenty of restorative sleep, and exercise. In any case, they were not regarded with the same suspicion as psychotic combatants, who were often accused of faking their condition in order to get pulled off the front lines.

Until recently, the historiography of modern warfare ignored tens of thousands of traumatized combatants, in particular those from the First World War.[9] Their pathologies were poorly diagnosed by their contemporaries, who attributed them to the shock from bombings, whence the name "shell shock," coined by British medical personnel. The French used the terms *obusite* (shell shock), *choc émotionnel* (emotional shock), and even *commotion* (concussion) interchangeably for the variety of nervous or psychic wounds the troops suffered.[10] But if thevocabulary is diverse—equal to the multiple forms of disturbance—the frequency of such pathologies was always explained the same way. Warfare and its violence were left largely blameless; the sick were "predisposed," the victims of a morbid heredity, and war only revealed or aggravated what was already there. An explanation that emerged during the conflict and prevailed at least until 1919, when it was officially proposed by the surgeon-general, a professor of experimental psychology named Georges Dumas,[11] and his psychiatric colleagues Antonin Porot and Angelo Hesnard, was that war "weighs seriously only on those whose mental state is already verging on imbalance, madness, or constitutional fragility."[12] It was hard for specialists to find warfare itself responsible when they viewed it as a test of virility, a kind of sink-or-swim for both body and soul. "Feminine" hysteria and nervousness were incompatible with the stereotype, yet these combat neuroses were now threatening to upset the norm.[13] Still, it was simpler to go with the notion of predisposition than to blame the war. People could then tell themselves that it was the enemy who was subject to such psychic delicacy—evidence of his weak constitution and, thus, his sure defeat.[14]

Given this ideological exoneration of war (a thesis that would be abandoned only gradually),[15] the sick could be seen as frauds. Throughout the conflict, the health service dreaded malingering and exaggerated its extent. In 1935, Drs. André Fribourg-Blanc and Marcel Gauthier were still insisting that many soldiers used "all available ruses and means to escape peril,"[16] a ruling in line with the continuing fantasy of fakers and exaggerators put forward by the medical corps, whose mission was to return men to the front as quickly as possible. The treatment of the mentally ill was directed at this single goal.

Accompanying the "gentle cure" Anthelme Mangin received in Bron in February 1918 were more coercive methods, including electroshock. This treatment had come into use in psychiatric centers and elsewhere before the war; it became prevalent, even systematic, during the war years, 1914 to 1918—a brutal method, wrote P. Chavigny but "efficient" if not "nearly infallible."[17] The physical pain was "always quite tolerable," according to Georges Dumas.[18] This was not the opinion of the patient who claimed to have received an electric shock strong enough to move a tram, adding that he would rather be court-martialed than relive the experience.[19] The goal of this torture (as some would call it) was to make patients want to emerge from their psychosis—the unconscious refuge of those who had chosen to flee the war.[20] If the malady became more difficult to endure than military service itself, then they would choose the horrors of the front over those of electroshock. Of course, they would not really have recovered, but every time the army would get one more soldier back, and that was what counted.

It is not known whether Mangin lost his senses on the battlefield, when he was wounded in the right leg and taken prisoner, or if he began to show signs of dementia in captivity. For if war can traumatize, so too can prison. The French medical profession would later coin the term *psychose des barbelés* (prisoner's syndrome) to describe the range of mental illnesses experienced by prisoners, while continuing to use the traditional and imprecise *cafard,* which could mean anything from passing gloom to suicidal depression. But in order for shell-shocked prisoners to receive the benefit of the Franco-German accord regarding repatriation of the wounded and the ill, the psychoses had first to be recognized, and the sick men no longer charged with faking or acting.

According to the Geneva Convention, nations at war must repatriate soldiers so ill or gravely wounded that they can no longer be expected to take part in the conflict. The Franco-German negotiations hit a snag, however, over whether to repatriate by individual or by category—as the French preferred, since they had far fewer prisoners than the Germans. It was only after the intervention of the Vatican and the president of the Helvetian Confederation that the first convoys of soldiers were exchanged, via Switzerland, in March 1915.[21] The Red Cross had to keep expanding its evacuations, which initially had been limited to the blind, amputees, and men with facial wounds. It even invented a classification of prisoners to be kept in Switzerland, which included the potentially curable. Not until May 1917 were those afflicted with the *psychose des barbelés* finally taken into account.[22] That was when Anthelme Mangin was added to the list of soldiers eligible for repatriation.

The civil service intake worker who completed the form for the unidentified man's hospitalization in Bron on February 1, 1918, took the trouble to add some question marks next to the name Anthelme Mangin, to indicate that he found the sick man's statements incoherent. When Mangin arrived at the asylum, without evacuation papers, the doctors knew nothing about his ailment. But the diagnosis was rapid: on February 23, Jean Lépine, the physician in charge of psychiatric services for the XIVth district as well as the director of the Rhône departmental asylums, stated that the patient in question was suffering from a "persecution complex" and "withdrawal," and should therefore be kept among the mentally disturbed.[23] The director of the Clermont-Ferrand asylum, where Mangin was soon sent, diagnosed "dementia praecox" and recommended that he be committed.[24] The medical certificate issued by A. Fenayrou, the director of the Rodez asylum, which Mangin entered on June 19, 1920, confirmed the ruling of his colleagues, but with more precision as to the subject's behavior: "Mental difficulties characterized at present by confused ideas, disorientation, complete unawareness, indifference to his situation, unconcern, total incapacity to care for himself. Incoherent language, answers with no relation to the questions asked; he stubbornly refuses to reply to questions regarding his identity. Extravagant gestures. Disorderly appearance. Mediocre general health. To be observed."[25] The symptoms he listed, from babbling to confusion, from indifference to rapidly alternating excitement and depression, are all part of what was known at the time as dementia praecox, which Fenayrou suspected but hesitated to diagnose. It is a progressive malady, characterized by disorientation in relation to time and space and manifests initially as excessive melancholy, leading to apathy, inertia, and reclusiveness. Symptoms include flat affect,[26] split personality, dreaminess, incoherence, whisperings, and the incomprehensible muddle of words that is, according to the psychiatrist Miloch Popovitch, "an adaptation of language to the feelings experienced in dreams."[27] The physical state eventually reflects the mental.

Progressive and incurable, dementia praecox is accompanied by the loss of memory, as it was in thirty-eight of the forty-one soldiers who were committed with the malady between 1914 and 1918 and who were still in treatment in 1926 in the Cadillac asylum,[28] in the southwestern department of Gironde. In reality, amnesia is rarely autonomous and is more easily understood as a secondary symptom, as Popovitch puts it, "contributing, with others, to the clinical expression of various affects."[29] Heterogeneous in its manifestation, it can be total or partial, permanent or temporary, delayed or retrograde,[30] but it is always fascinating for medical personnel. The war made the condition so common that as early as 1915 it was attracting the attention of specialists[31]— a double-edged interest, because, as with all mental disturbances of the period, the sick soldiers were suspected of faking. "We believe there is no intellectual disturbance as frequently and easily simulated as amnesia," Dr. Jules Perret stated in 1919.[32] However, recognizing that "the simulator is rarely a normal person,"[33] he agreed with Freud, for whom "all neurotics are fakers; they simulate without knowing it, and that is their illness."[34]

Their treatment for amnesia was not simple. As Louis Régis explained in 1920, the doctors had to restore the patient's confidence with gentle care while taking pains to avoid the "caresses" and "unnecessary pampering" that might allow the amnesiac to find comfort in his affliction.[35] Fresh air, sunshine, baths, exercise: all these were called for, plus a detoxifying regimen of purgatives, diuretics, or stomach pumping, on the theory that it is necessary to expel the evil—an approach in reality not so very far removed from the practice of bleeding, which had fallen out of use a century earlier.[36] Not all medical personnel were convinced of the virtues of such treatment, though, and some called for another approach. Based on the accepted understanding of regression, whereby in amnesia the destruction of memory follows a logical pattern, first erasing recent memories and then, more slowly, earlier ones, these specialists imagined that in focusing on "dominant memories"—the ones most charged with feeling (intimacies, tragedies, passions, marriage, children, grief)— they could break down the patient's psychic armor.[37] They theorized that amnesia is always partial and that the memory's fabric can be repaired via the fundamentals that organize even the memories of sick people. The way to proceed, they thought, was through establishing connections, evoking situations, questioning, and encouraging the family to recall the most important moments in the amnesiac's life. But this method could work only with patients actually seeking to recover their memories. Mangin had no such desire, and thus he foiled the work of those trying to identify him.

Questioned upon his entry into the Rhône departmental asylum in Bron on February 1, 1918, the unidentified man gave his name as Anthelme Mangin, his birth date as March 1 (he did not know the year), and his residence as rue Sélastras in Vichy. There were no more questions, and he waited to be transferred to the Clermont-Ferrand asylum, which was closer to where he apparently was from, once a convoy of soldiers repatriated from Germany was ready to leave for the Auvergne.

The transfer took place on March 22. Mangin entered the private Sainte-Marie-de-l'Assomption asylum in Clermont-Ferrand, and an investigation was launched in Vichy.

It was quickly determined that rue Sélastras did not exist there and that Anthelme Mangin was completely unknown. The hoax the patient had pulled on the authorities high-lighted an aspect of his behavior and of his affliction: he absolutely refused to allow himself to be identified, sending doctors on wild-goose chases and inventing names and addresses out of whole cloth in order to cut short the interrogations, which he hated. His unconscious wish was to be left in peace, unidentified. The doctors spoke of this syndrome as "negativist" amnesia, a relatively rare disturbance with few prospects for a cure.[38] Fenayrou, the director of the Aveyron departmental asylum in Rodez, confirmed the diagnosis in November 1920: "His behavior when he is asked questions of this sort leads me to believe that his silence and false replies are not due to a loss of memory but are, rather, manifestations of reticence originating in delirium."[39] By that time Anthelme Mangin, interned in Rodez since June 19, had repeated his stunt, embarrassing Fenayrou. Four days after his arrival at the asylum, Fenayrou had met with him at length and interrogated him, calmly but insistently, until the patient cracked and revealed his identity, twice—once in writing. Fenayrou immediately alerted the Aveyron prefect to his success and asked for a prompt follow-up:

> I am pleased to report that today, as a result of my persistence,
> I succeeded in getting this man to answer the questions I

asked him regarding his name, his age, and his place of birth. According to his statements, he is named Mongin Adrien, is approximately thirty years old, and was born in Chartres.[40]

Aware, however, that his colleague in Bron had been duped, Fenayrou did not yet claim victory: "There is nothing less certain than that this information is correct." And in fact the investigation that the prefect of Eure-et-Loir undertook brought no more satisfaction than the one in Vichy had.[41] Once again, Mangin had bested his caretakers. Fenayrou's misadventure might have been amusing had Mangin not been so oblivious. But it did give fodder to journalists, one of whom characterized the amnesiac as a cynic "who, in going mad, has willingly entered into a kind of living death out of disgust with murderous humanity, the way one used to discover religion out of love's loss."[42] Marcel Nadaud and Maurice Pelletier, of *Le Petit Journal,* went even further and wrote that the patient, when asked to sign a document, had, with great irony, signed the name Lenin.[43]

The truth was sadder. Mangin had no sense of irony at all. He was merely a soldier who had fled the war and his own identity. In his condition, it was useless to attempt to reeducate him or even to identify him from his own statements. As for the journalistic fantasies that described brutal attempts to awaken Mangin with flashing lights, or to interrogate the poor amnesiac to the point of exhaustion,[44] it was better for all concerned to ignore them.

In any case, the director of the Clermont-Ferrand asylum was quite put out when he learned that Mangin had given a false address in Bron. He notified his colleague in Bron, who then, on October 10, 1918, requested help from the information office of the Ministry of War. This branch of the administration replied on November 9 that they knew nothing of Mangin, about whom no inquiries had been made, and called for an investigation—which made no progress at all until the patient's photograph appeared in the newspapers in February 1922.[45] In the meantime, Mangin remained at Clermont-Ferrand, wearing the standard uniform of the incurably insane. He was not the only veteran who remained unidentified; but gradually, whether through death, or recognition by families, or chance identification,[46] their numbers diminished: there were ten at the beginning of 1919, only six a year later. Their photographs and descriptions were posted in offices throughout Paris, in Les Invalides, and in regional centers, but the general public knew little of them.

On December 23, 1919, the daily *Le Petit Parisien* ran what seems to have been the first article about them for the general public. It was brief, and what it reported was simple: that a number of amnesiac soldiers who remained unidentified were interned in asylums. In the following days, *Le Petit Parisien* received many letters from relatives of soldiers gone missing, requesting that the paper publish the photographs of these unfortunate men. On January 10, 1920, the paper reprinted six photographs for its hundreds of thousands of readers in the hope that the pictures would be recognized and "that their publication would keep painful uncertainties and disappointments from being prolonged."[47] The accompanying descriptions included such things as scars, tattoos, regional accents, hair color, height, and dental condition. But Mangin was rather undistinguished. His eyes, his brown mustache and hair, his pale skin, and his five-foot-four-and-a-half-inch height were common—and that was perhaps the source of his drama. For many, many families would claim to recognize Anthelme Mangin as a lost relative. Most of them changed their minds once they saw a clearer picture forwarded by the asylum. Others, borne on by hope, made the trip to see Mangin, like one family from Nantes in May 1920. Mme. Delafouilhousse de Péchadoire, from Puy-de-Dôme, was certain: the crazed soldier she visited was certainly the son whose death she had been refusing to accept for years—a conviction she would stand by until the middle of the twenties, despite the contrary conclusion of an expert in 1923. But at the beginning of 1920, she made the mistake of failing to launch legal proceedings to claim the amnesiac, leaving the field open for Mme. Mazenc and her daughter, Louise Vayssettes, of Aveyron, to try to have the unknown man awarded to them.

Before the war, Albert Mazenc had lived in Vors, a small town near Rodez, where he worked as a wheelwright. Born August 13, 1877, in Sauveterre, a town in Courbenac, he was a widower raising a ten-year-old son and a six-year-old daughter on his own when war broke out in August 1914[48]— which was why he was not initially drafted. But he was inducted soon enough, in 1915, as the country sought every means to end draft dodging in its effort to raise new troops for the ongoing conflict. Mazenc, assigned to the 342nd Infantry, disappeared at Tahure on October 30, 1915.[49] Because none of his comrades saw him fall, his mother and sister refused to accept his death. On January 10, 1920, they both thought they recognized him in the photograph of Anthelme Mangin. The sister, Louise Vayssettes, a Rodez laundress who had taken in her missing brother's two children, journeyed to Clermont-Ferrand, and arriving at the Sainte-Marie asylum she was categorical: there could be no doubt that the unidentified No. 13 and Albert Mazenc were one and the same man. She immediately sought to have her rights legally recognized— by pleading her cause before the Rodez branch of the League for the Rights of Man, before veterans' groups, and especially before the Aveyron prefect.

On April 22, the prefect agreed to the Mazenc-Vayssettes plea, which sought the transfer of the Clermont-Ferrand amnesiac to Rodez, and he intervened accordingly with his counterpart in Puy-de-Dôme.[50] Following an exchange of letters, and allowing time for the families who thought they had recognized Mangin in *Le Petit Parisien* to see him and acknowledge their error, the Puy-de-Dôme prefect approved the transfer on June 10. On June 19, Anthelme Mangin entered the Rodez asylum. The establishment was not among the best equipped. It was small and sheltered far more mentally ill patients than it was supposed to—built for 400, it housed more than 600.[51] Between 1914 and 1919, some 115 soldiers had been committed there, and when Mangin entered, it still housed 49 veterans for whom the war had never ended. Fenayrou, the author of a study of insanity in the department of Aveyron,[52] had been the director there since 1912; he reached the top level of his civil-service rank in November 1919.[53] A small asylum in the heart of a remote, rural department, the Rodez asylum was not exactly a prestige post, but Fenayrou lived a calm and predictable life there (one of his benefits was free utilities)—until Mangin arrived. Thrust into the spotlight from 1922 to 1937, Fenayrou became so entirely focused on the amnesiac that ultimately he was unable to conduct the institution's daily business. (In March 1930, he secured a special bonus for himself and his assistant to compensate them for the excess work—endless research and verifications—related to Mangin's identification.[54])

In 1920, the laundress of Rodez was the only person officially claiming the amnesiac. The government had acted in her favor in authorizing Mangin's transfer to the Aveyron departmental asylum, and it was with this trump card in hand that, on August 23, she requested guardianship of the patient. The reply was slow in coming. She wrote again to the Aveyron prefect on December 3 and 5: "A deeply saddened family calls upon your sense of justice to recognize our rights." Citing Mangin's sweet nature, she pointed out that he was not dangerous and could easily leave the asylum and join her family, adding that her brother was not mad, merely amnesiac, and that he would certainly recover once he was in the comfort of his own home. Being a woman of modest means, her sole request was to benefit in return from Mangin's pension—which was only just, of course, because if he was declared her brother, she would lose the orphan's pensions of the two Mazenc children she had taken in in 1915. Her letter was signed by practically the entire family of Albert Mazenc, sisters and brothers, mother and sisters-in-law—with one exception. Jean-Baptiste

Mazenc, one of Albert's brothers, withheld his signature, refusing to recognize the amnesiac. His sister tried to explain away his disavowal by calling him a liar "who pretends not to recognize the patient on the basis that he no longer has all his faculties";[55] even before Mangin's transfer from Clermont-Ferrand to Rodez, this heartless peasant had declared, in front of witnesses, "I don't want any lunatic in our house. . . . If he's an imbecile, he's better off staying in Clermont-Ferrand—better than having him here."[56] When Jean-Baptiste Mazenc saw Mangin in Rodez, it took him less than fifteen minutes to confirm his skepticism definitively.

This family disagreement raised doubts in the mind of Fenayrou, whom the Aveyron prefect had consulted regarding Louise Vayssettes's plea. On September 7, Fenayrou cautioned the prefect against acting "lightly" or "hurriedly" in awarding Mangin to "strangers," because "neither Mme. Vayssettes nor her mother can prove that the patient in question is truly her brother or son."[57] The resemblance alone was not sufficient proof for Fenayrou, who wanted tangible evidence before developing an opinion; but he did not shut the door on the Mazencs, hoping they would keep visiting Mangin in the asylum and working with him to establish proof of their relationship and (maybe it wasn't too much to hope for) to awaken repressed memories in the patient. The prefect's decision, on September 9, followed this line of thinking. While not yet winning legal guardianship of Mangin, Mme. Vayssettes did win the right to visit him twice a week, and she made her visits regularly, accompanied most often by Maria

Mazenc, Albert's daughter.[58] Even after 1923, when she ultimately failed in her quest for legal guardianship, she would continue to make the twice-weekly visits, bringing the amnesiac sweets and small presents. (The visits were reduced to once weekly in 1927, owing to the endless examinations Mangin was then receiving and his resulting overstimulation.)[59]

Despite the legal setback, the Mazenc-Vayssettes's chances were not to be counted out. But another blow came in the form of motions on August 8 and October 7, 1920, by Mme. Delafouilhousse, objecting to their winning guardianship of the man she was convinced was her son. Then, in November, one E. Mangin, living in Vichy, wrote to Fenayrou requesting a photograph of the unidentified man on behalf of a relative seeking her child. This news aroused so much enthusiasm that the prefect notified Emile Allon, inspector-general at the Ministry of Pensions, who in turn expressed his hopes: "There is a curious coincidence between the request for information made by M. E. Mangin of Vichy and the fact that the patient at first identified himself as being from that city."[60] But the curious coincidence turned out to be nothing more than that, as the Mangin in Vichy returned the photo without shedding any light on the identity of the Mangin in Rodez. Still, a decision had to be made, and the Aveyron prefect, the Minister of Pensions, and Fenayrou were resolved to find a prompt solution that would suit everyone.

The Mazencs and Vayssetteses were almost certainly not Mangin's family. But because they claimed him so fiercely, it seemed likely that they would treat him properly, and with love, so why not give him to them? This was Fenayrou's position in November 1920, when he went so far as to propose implementation of the following action:

> I do not believe that the present state of affairs should continue indefinitely. And if our investigations remain inconclusive, it would seem suitable, at a certain point, to give Mme. Vayssettes and her mother satisfaction by making them responsible for the care and upkeep of the sick man, even if their relationship to him has not been established absolutely.[61]

The director of the Rodez asylum was no fool. He had never completely accepted the Vayssetteses' theory, and by this time he knew for certain that Mangin and Mazenc were two different men. In October, with the aid of the commander of the Rodez recruiting office, he had procured a description of Albert Mazenc. The soldier was just over five feet tall, some four inches less than Anthelme Mangin; it was hardly likely that Mazenc, who was thirty-seven in 1914, had continued to grow during the war. So then it was not a question of the director's recognizing the amnesiac as Albert Mazenc but rather of the sick man's being placed in the care of an unrelated family—a common enough practice—after the moral character of the family had been established and the living conditions cleared. The director's position, which he reaffirmed on December 15, was his final one, provided that no other leads turned up anything. Emile Allon, at the Ministry of Pensions, agreed: "I believe that the resolution of this problem lies in placing the ill man with the Vayssettes family, under the conditions laid out by the asylum director."[62] On

December 10, the official in charge of the file at the Ministry of Pensions, one Valentino, ordered a final investigation to determine whether the unidentified man should be turned over to Mme. Vayssettes. To this end, the Rodez police commissioner was asked to evaluate the family's moral character and circumstances: "Your conclusions [will be] the basis of my decision," the prefect wrote to him.[63] On December 23, the commissioner sent back a favorable report: M. Vayssettes was an honest working man, and his wife, née Mazenc, who owned a laundry, was a goodhearted woman who had taken in her brother's children when he was drafted, in 1915. The case of the Rodez amnesiac—the last vestige of the war—was on the verge of being put to rest, if not resolved, by this convenient solution.

Unfortunately, the good woman went too far. A campaign by a large veterans' group was encouraging the minister to decide for the Mazencs, but a deputy (that is, a member of the French parliament) named Raynaldy, brought in toward the end of 1920 to carry the day, turned out to be a two-edged sword. Not doubting the strength of Louise Vayssettes's case, since nearly the whole family had made the identification, Raynaldy proposed one final meeting with those who had known Albert Mazenc; after this formality, any lingering doubts on the ministry's part would certainly disappear. The prefect agreed to this final step, and on January 4, 1921, he called together everyone likely to be able to identify Albert Mazenc. On January 6, a teacher named Marty, a property owner from the town of Vors, and a mechanic came to the asylum. They were followed on January 8 by a farmer, and

finally by the mayor of Vors himself. All declared without hesitation that the patient was not Mazenc. His height and the
color of his hair were different; Mangin spoke only French,
while Albert Mazenc spoke a patois; and Mangin neither
stuttered like Mazenc nor bore his tattoo. Although Joseph
Mazenc and Mme. Béral, Albert's brother and sister, protested
that when they visited, the patient "did speak patois when the
occasion called for it" and that he could have grown since the
military medical examination, their assertions rang false.
Louise Vayssettes protested vigorously as well, claiming to
have heard the patient speak patois and denouncing those
who failed to recognize her brother as having been influenced
by Jean-Baptiste Mazenc's continuing disagreement with his
family. Nevertheless, there was no longer any doubt: Mangin
was not Mazenc. The ministry backed off from handing over
the amnesiac to Mme. Vayssettes.[64] A final intervention by the
president of the Rodez branch of the League of the Rights of
Man, on November 7, 1921, met with no more success.
Though he did not believe the man to be Albert Mazenc, he
felt, "in the name of humanity" and given that family life
could only benefit the amnesiac, that the patient would be
better off among those who loved him as one of their own
than in a madhouse. The principle was clear, and Fenayrou
did not disagree. But before acceding, he felt that one last effort to identify Mangin had to be made.

On December 15, 1920, the director of the asylum had proposed that the Aveyron prefect appeal to the minister of
health and the minister of pensions to publish the amnesiac's

photo in the largest national newspapers. If this final attempt bore no fruit, then and only then would they have to seriously consider awarding the patient to the Vayssettes. The prefect complied, but the Ministry of Pensions did not react favorably, as it had already tried this tack in *Le Petit Parisien* the previous January, with disappointing results.

Before contacting the supervisor of disputes at the Ministry of Pensions, the prefect, in his capacity as the state's representative, had made inquiries about the investigation already opened in October 1918 by the Ministry of War.[65] It was hardly worth the bother: in two years, nothing at all had been done. The minister of health, welfare, and state insurance, to whom he wrote on March 12, 1921,[66] was no more helpful. This minister, who oversaw the guardianship of Mangin, was sour on the whole idea of publishing the picture, which he thought would only complicate matters by multiplying the number of families claiming the patient. So he confined himself to formally encouraging further efforts at identification,[67] without acknowledging that such efforts were pointless so long as Mangin's face remained unseen. On April 19, the prefect, observing to him that there was nothing new in the case, pleaded passionately for going ahead with the plan of publicizing the amnesiac's story. With so much disagreement within the hierarchy, things ground to a halt.

On June 13, the prefect, as conscientious as he was stubborn, reiterated his request. This time, the director of disputes, Valentino, cut short the evasions and silences of his ministry: "It does not appear necessary that my department publish the picture of the interned man in the large newspapers with a view toward establishing his identity."[68] The case was closed, the reply cutting. But for the prefect, the tragedy of an unknown soldier and a family crying out, however mistakenly, for their missing brother or husband was intolerable. On November 9, he once again called on the minister of health, begging him to force his colleague to authorize publication of the photograph: even if it turned up no one new, they had to do everything in their power to discover poor Mangin's true identity—it was a question of duty and honor for the French administration, which should not open itself to later accusations "of having covered up the existence of the missing man." Given the stubbornness of the Ministry of Pensions, the affair would have ended there, had Mangin not also been the center of a financial imbroglio that would lead the civil authorities to look into his case.

Under the military pensions law, Anthelme Mangin—like every French soldier wounded or disabled in war since February 27, 1793—was entitled to a pension. The invention of national war had impelled the French Revolutionary government to establish just compensation for soldier-citizens crippled in the name of their country. When France went to war in August 1914, pensions for wounded and disabled soldiers were operating according to the law of April 2, 1831, which divided infirmities into six classes. (The insane were classified in the fourth.) To be eligible, one had to offer proof of the date the malady was contracted or the combat wound suffered.[69] The law was too rigid to suit modern warfare, and so the government created an extraparliamentary commission charged with rewriting it by the end of 1915. The insane—a large group incapable of doing anything to advance their own cause—came under the wing of the doctors charged with considering the question of benefits.[70] On March 31, 1919, the Chamber of Deputies finally voted in the Lugol plan, a synthesis of the five plans the extraparliamentary commission had developed. Under its terms, a disabled veteran no longer had to prove much of anything, and any crippling disease contracted up to six months after returning home would be covered as the result of battle trauma. The pension was automatic for the mentally ill, but it was difficult to establish the percentage of disability, because mental illnesses were so varied and so ill defined. For his part, Anthelme Mangin was in the maximum-benefits category. For mentally ill veterans interned in psychiatric centers, a simple certificate signed by the doctor in charge was all the consulting medical committee needed to grant maximum benefits.[71] The Rodez amnesiac did present one problem, though: having no identity, he could not receive benefits. Owing to this simple fact, no part of the French administration recognized Mangin, and he was therefore no one's responsibility.

From the moment Mangin entered the Rodez asylum, Fenayrou worried over who was going to pay for this troublesome soul's care, since he was covered by the Ministry of War only temporarily. The doctor asked for clarification from his counterpart in Clermont-Ferrand, who told him that the rules committee had not adjudicated Mangin's case because he had no identity. On August 17, 1920, Fenayrou formulated a request for a pension from the health service in the XVIth

District (Montpellier) on behalf of his patient. On November 4, the Rodez commission awarded him a temporary full pension, and on November 27 he was discharged from the army. But his discharge was hardly a solution; now he was neither on the army's rolls nor anybody else's, and so his pension never began. This turn of events infuriated Fenayrou, who was left with the expense of Mangin's care.[72] In an effort to rectify such an absurd—and financially draining—situation, Fenayrou pressed the general paymaster of pensions of the XVIth District to have his ministry take responsibility for the patient. On June 2 and 8 and September 17, 1921, Fenayrou reiterated his plea, without success. For its part, the department of Aveyron refused to consider Mangin as an indigent and therefore to cover the cost of his care at the asylum.[73] However, with the help of Senator Joseph Monsservin, a plan to force the ministry to assume its responsibilities was put into place.

On December 30, 1921, during the second session of the Senate, a veritable ambush awaited André Maginot, the minister of pensions. Monsservin, a jurist from the Rodez establishment who had served as senator from Aveyron since 1912 (when he replaced his father, Emile),[74] and was also president of the Aveyron general council, cleverly took advantage of the Upper Assembly's debate on the pensions budget to force Maginot into a decision. After dealing with purely financial questions, the debate had turned to the problem of the transfer of bodies, specifically of those prisoners who had died in Germany and whose families wished to reclaim them. It was at this moment that Monsservin interrupted the discussion:

Gentlemen, I, too, am concerned with prisoners of war, but in an infinitely more miserable category than those gloriously dead on foreign soil.

I am speaking of prisoners brought back to France and interned in insane asylums without having been identified. This handful of former soldiers—and I realize there are very few, but even if there were only one it would be too many—seems to have been permanently abandoned, crossed off the lists of the living, left in a deafening silence and, with that silence, oblivion. And yet there are families somewhere in France to whom they belong, inconsolable families who believe them dead.

We have sought help, M. Minister of Pensions, from those serving under you, who have replied that they are not competent to proceed with efforts to identify these unknown soldiers, and who, for reasons I find unreasonable, have declined to publish the photographs provided them: because they feel that the families to whom these prisoners may belong might experience suffering when they learn of the diminished mental state in which their children are languishing.

And the doors of insane asylums, like those of Dante's Inferno, remain locked, without any trace of hope!

Where it is a question of improving, of easing the living conditions of these disabled veterans by giving them, or the care facilities where they are committed, the pensions they have coming to them—pensions that were approved by the rules committee—your ministry has pronounced: "We do not know these soldiers' identities. Therefore we cannot award them a pension or a temporary status, nor any help whatsoever, as our pensions must be attached to a name." As a result, we now find ourselves at an unacceptable impasse. To the request "Identify them" you respond, "We are not competent to do so." To "At least give them some kind of pension!" you answer, "But we don't know them."

I am persuaded, M. Minister, that you are unaware of this narrow and inhumane interpretation of the law. Too well I know your sense of fairness, too well I know your attachment to your own former fellow soldiers to think for a moment that you would leave in such moral and financial distress those who have fought for France, and who left behind them, along with the horrors of battle or captivity, if not their lives, then their very senses.

You must hasten to pursue their identification by all means possible. Every day lost can only further complicate matters. Families who could be consoled must not be allowed to despair, nor—and I draw your attention to this point especially—can new marriages be sealed based on the certainty that these men have died.

It is thus urgent to order a new search. The photographs can be sent to associations of the disabled or other veterans' groups. The large newspapers will, I am sure, devote columns to making these men known to the public. It is an act of sacred patriotism that none will refuse.

The Senate, M. Minister, awaits your attention to this unfortunate matter. I beg the pardon of my colleagues for having brought this situation to their attention in the midst of budget discussions, but it is never a waste of time to pause for those most unfortunate—especially where our soldiers are concerned—and to find a solution.[75]

Monsservin's brilliant speech, vigorously applauded by his colleagues, convinced the minister to agree to his demands and authorize a search for the amnesiacs' relatives via the press. "Although such publicity may have undesired consequences, I am ready to try it," he replied.[76] As for the problem of their pensions, he stated that his ministry, in collaboration with the Ministry of Finance, was already examining the question of whether a pension might be issued to an assumed name, a number, or a code (an idea that quietly died). But, he continued, while awaiting a resolution to this troubling problem of allocating names to disability pensions, he would proceed with reimbursement of expenses advanced by the asylums for the care of these unidentified insane veterans.[77] "Accordingly," he concluded, "from this moment forward, and even before the pensions are officially awarded, reimbursement as requested will be available for the departmental asylums in question." The members of parliament approved—"Very good! Very good!"—and Monsservin thanked the minister. The contretemps over who would pay for the amnesiacs' care was settled. But Mangin's fate was also sealed.

From the moment the tragedy of these deranged and interned veterans became known in the December 30 session, the press was enamored of the "poor lunatics," "living unknown soldiers" whose families were mourning them as dead. January to March 1922 saw numerous articles published about them. One of the first, in *L'Echo national,* a newspaper founded by Georges Clemenceau, virulently attacked the Ministry of Pensions for having done too little to identify them; the paper also appropriated as its own the idea of publishing photographs of the "six anonymous victims of this most horrifying of wars" in the national press.[78] On January 11, 1922, *L'Echo national* announced that its solemn call had been heard: the ministry was now disposed to publish the photographs and descriptions of the lunatics. The paper also claimed the task of identifying three of the six amnesiacs Monsservin had mentioned in his speech before the Senate on December 30, warning readers who wanted to know more, however, that it would publish the photographs in question only as a last recourse, "in order to avoid such painful mistakes in identification as have already occurred in this situation."[79] In reality it could not have published the photographs before the other papers even had it wanted to, because the ministry was set to release them to all the newspapers at the same time. On February 5, *La Voix du combattant,* the newspaper of the National Veterans Union, believing the information would arrive imminently, announced that "as there is no question of doing sensational reporting in such painful circumstances, the union of Parisian and departmental newspapers and the newspapers of organizations for the disabled and for veterans will all receive the documents on the same day, and all newspapers will be asked to publish them the exact same day, if possible."[80]

The pretensions of *L'Echo national* were widely copied. Before long, practically every newspaper was congratulating itself for having been the first to throw light on the subject. On February 19, *La Voix du combattant* touted itself, under the byline of the Veterans Union's national secretary, Deputy

Charles Bertrand, on being the first newspaper to publish pictures of the unidentified men, meanwhile insisting that the achievement was not a matter of pride but rather "the accomplishment of a sacred duty."[81] On the same day, the pictures of the amnesiacs appeared in several other publications, including *Le Matin,* one of the largest national newspapers.[82] *Le Petit journal* had nevertheless gotten the jump on them all the day before by printing the photographs (rather discreetly on page 3), without the accompanying descriptions, as soon as it received them.[83] In 1931, *Le Journal des mutilés et combattants* was priding itself on having been the first to write about the Anthelme Mangin case, even though in 1922 it had not published his picture until February 25.[84] Similarly, in 1937 Paul Bringuier claimed to have originated the expression "the living unknown soldier"—a claim that Jean Anouilh seconded in his drama[85]—when in fact in 1922 the press was generally calling the men "the living unknown vets." But such vanities were of little real importance. They are easily explained by the sense of tragedy surrounding these men, the sense of an urgent need to deal with a pressing duty. The newspapers unanimously considered the presentation of this dramatic story a "sacred duty," an "act of sacred patriotism" (in Senator Monsservin's phrase)—a necessary and spontaneous show of national solidarity: "In our country, one never calls upon humanity in vain."[86]

The duty was threefold. First, it applied to the amnesiacs themselves, the traumatized soldiers who were not just called "miserable vets"[87] out of pity but were considered comrades by other veterans: "Having gone through the same harsh trials that left our comrades in such dire circumstances, veterans are in a better position than anyone else to empathize."[88] Taking up the task of identifying the sick men, veterans thus celebrated their fraternity in a mixture of patriotism and love of humanity that was far removed from the official patriotism they generally deplored.[89] They saw the amnesiacs as victims ("anonymous victims" according to *L'Echo national,* "the most doleful victims of the war" for the organ of the National Veterans Union) and also as heroes: "We owe so much to those whose heroism allowed France to emerge victorious from the international torment that put its very existence at stake."[90] At a time when most memorials were being erected for heroes who had died for France, and not for victims incapable of making known the grandeur of their sacrifice,[91] these nameless madmen were a curious synthesis: heroes who, reduced to a pitiful state, incarnated the suffering of France.

For this reason, the duty the newspapers were invoking was, second, a duty toward families in mourning. The martyrdom of these men unaware either of what had happened to them or of anything around them was nothing, after all, next to the grief of the families who were all too aware as they mourned the loss of their loved ones. The men and women of a France that had veiled itself in black, torn asunder by the individual and collective mourning for some 1,400,000 dead and missing men, were too familiar with the pain of loss to discount the emotion that the discovery of three amnesiac veterans dredged up. "And if it were my son, my husband, my brother, my comrade?" asked everyone who had never given up hope. In the name of the families of France and of national sentiment," *L'Echo national* sought to "dry the tears" of relatives[92] and to deliver them "from the most tragic uncertainty."[93]

Finally, the most miserable citizens were not those who knew that their soldiers were dead. The duty to discover an identity for the men with no names was, above all, the duty to halt any grotesquely mistaken mourning for a missing person who might still be alive:

> France lost 1,500,000 men, but only 1,100,000 families are able to mourn at gravesides, for 400,000 soldiers were declared missing, their bodies destroyed in the firestorm. Well, one of these 400,000 mournings is in error. Somewhere in France, in some village, on the column of a war monument somewhere, one name is engraved that should not be there.[94]

One could wonder whether it was not something more than the desire to assuage the grief of families that aroused such emotion and fascination around these unidentified men. Having come back from the war but still hopelessly removed from the world of the living, the deranged soldiers had something in common with those who had not returned. *Le Journal des mutilés et combattants* of February 25 somewhat confusedly formulated this sentiment when it headlined an article "The Living Dead." So it was that the dehumanized amnesiacs became emblems of both the country's suffering and the bereft families who deserved to be honored and assisted—something Paul Bringuier well understood when he compared the mad Mangin to the Unknown Soldier:

Under the Arc de Triomphe at l'Etoile, a flame burns on the tomb of the Unknown Soldier, the symbol of a sacrifice made by all. But somewhere in the depths of a madhouse, the Unknown Soldier has a living comrade who embodies the same symbol—he, too, the phantom of an era, the miraculous earthly representative of 400,000 French soldiers whose sacrificial humility was such that they left no remains whatsoever.[95]

Anthelme Mangin, a living dead man, a ghostly symbol of grief, aroused in his contemporaries a tragic fascination with a story that had only begun.

Chapter Two

The Impossible Grief for the Missing

There is no way really to understand the passion the Anthelme Mangin affair stirred in the French without looking
deeply into the drama of the missing, and of the hundreds of
thousands of relatives who scrutinized photographs of the
Rodez amnesiac for resemblances to the young men whose
deaths they could never accept. The missing, silent when roll
was called after an assault, neither officially killed nor physically present, the half-alive, half-dead, might always return at
any moment. A letter from a prisoner-of-war camp somewhere in Germany might end the anguish in a burst of joy.
But when weeks, months of silence went by, it became more
and more likely that these unmournable dead had found their
final resting place in no-man's-land. No body, no tomb, no
death—how could anyone accept it? The traditional experience of death was unsettled by a new kind of warfare that
swallowed up individuals and left their loved ones back at

home in endless uncertainty. The number of soldiers who were never to return, either dead or alive, was enormous: in November 1915, after the carnage of the first months of the war (the most casualty-heavy),[1] they were already estimated at 300,000[2]—a number not that much lower than the 350,000[3] reported in May 1919 by the national commission on war cemeteries. Using as a sample just the 126 families who asked to meet Anthelme Mangin and gave the date of their relative's loss in their correspondence with Fenayrou, the first two years of the war took the greatest toll: two-thirds of the men sought had gone missing in 1914 and 1915.[4]

The heaviest losses came in 1914, with the largest contingent going missing in August and September[5]—a period that marked not only the most violent phase of the action but, especially, the French retreat, which while not precipitous did not allow for retrieval of bodies from the battlefield. On their side, the Germans, rushing to advance, counted the scattered corpses only roughly. Hence the high number of missing in the first weeks of the war. This situation continued with the repeated offensives of the following year. The high number of soldiers left on the ground between the trenches and the resulting absence of bodies, or of identity tags taken from bodies, forced the military authorities to accept the word of comrades in establishing records for death certificates. The number of missing diminished in the war's remaining years.

Before the war broke out, precautions had been taken to avoid this loss of bodies and identities. Every soldier was equipped with a metal tag bearing his first and last name and date of induction on one side, and his registration number on the other. These tags, hung from the neck and worn under the shirt, could be removed from dead soldiers and the information transmitted to their families through the intermediary of local city halls, which were to issue the death certificates. Nothing was left to chance. But the system, which even charged health officials with the burials, worked only so long as the French were winning. The retreat of 1914 prevented the retrieval and burial of the dead, and the steadiness of the rout thwarted the plans for emergency care. Frequently men had to be buried rapidly, sometimes feverishly, by their comrades, on the spot where they died, or in groups, in makeshift ditches next to the trenches.

The enemy's firepower was clearly what caused the phenomenon of the missing. Buried alive, dismembered, vaporized by heavy artillery, many soldiers "took up less space in their caskets than their names did on their dog tags."[6] Many more who died in no-man's-land were never recovered by their comrades; why risk more lives retrieving corpses? At best, the dead could be exhumed should the territory be retaken.

Sometimes, though, units received orders to foray out to retrieve and bury the dead—at night, of course, to limit the risk. Cpl. Louis Barthas, remembering this "drudgery," described the horrible rummaging around the bodies to find dog tags as a desecration and a "grim duty," especially when the corpses were "half-squashed, mangled, caked with dirt, tangled in equipment, packs, bags, no longer much of anything but muddy, bloody heaps."[7] If Barthas, on the front lines, complained about having neither water nor a washcloth for his hands, farther back the same revulsion for decomposing bodies persisted even under less crude conditions. To an officer named Paul Truffeau, who voiced concern about the number of anonymous graves, a soldier replied: "Ten days went by before we could bury them, and when we got there to do it, the stench was terrible. The men worked with handkerchiefs around their faces and with gloves. They would dig a ditch and then snag the corpse by the neck with a kind of hook and pull him in."[8] Some soldiers were in less of a hurry; they managed to overcome their revulsion out of duty or feelings of kinship with the dead and their anguished families back home. For Capt. Ferdinand Belmont, this "atrocious task," this "doleful labor," was an act of faith from which one could not shrink:

> From time to time, when digging a tunnel, a shovel would turn up a half-buried body. You couldn't always tell if it was a German or a Frenchman—it was only something rotten, a thing with no name. Yet sometimes we tried to identify the thing. Ignoring your revulsion, you might find a paper, a letter, a folder. Who else would do it later? And the thought of all the sorrow created by uncertainty helped you make the effort.[9]

As for the bodies of comrades who fell between the front lines, collecting them and giving them a decent burial and even a simple ceremony was a duty, a necessary show of solidarity, reminding the soldiers of their own deaths, conjuring up the horror of dying alone, like an animal, without the final ritual of the grave or the rites that define us as human. To limit the chances of an anonymous death, this kind of solidarity became automatic: "Each person did it naturally, knowing that if the man next to you was cut down today, tomorrow perhaps it would be your turn, and the survivors would honor your remains as you had others'."[10] Similarly, it was the survivors' duty to inform the family about a comrade's death and final resting place, so that one day he could be exhumed and returned home.[11] The wretchedness of soldiers in invaded territory— terrified at the idea of dying away from their families' tears, without anyone's knowing how they had died or where their remains moldered—was the worst. Whom could their comrades even write to, when they were cut off from communication, isolated? A substantial number found the solution in an institution created specifically for them, and one whose success quickly altered the big picture: war godmothers. Extracts of letters published by Henriette de Vismes, a Catholic activist who collaborated in the first of such activities, in *La Famille du soldat* (*The Soldier's Family*), showed how much veterans wanted to leave some kind of message for their families:

> Often I feel discouraged because . . . if I die, no one will hear about it, and when the country is liberated, my mother won't know where I fell or if I behaved well.[12]
>
> I'm asking you if it's possible to tell my mother after the war that her son died bravely, because whatever it takes, I'll do my duty to the end. Here is my mother's address. . . . [13]

What most preoccupied soldiers when they thought about the terrible possibility of going missing was the desire for someone to find and bury their body. So it was that the mayor of Anguilcourt-le-Sart, executed in 1915 by occupying forces after the discovery that his village had been hiding two soldiers since September 1914, described, in his last letter from prison, the clothes he was wearing and mentioned the glasses tucked in the pocket, so that one day someone could identify him and place his body in the family tomb.[14]

In any case, the conditions under which soldiers gathered up bodies between the trenches—hastily, nocturnally, fearful of enemy fire and revolted at the necessity of touching bodies in advanced states of decay—inevitably meant that the searches were superficial. They were even more so when the bodies belonged to German soldiers. Despite General Command directives that just as much effort be made to identify enemy dead—whose names could then be exchanged for those of French soldiers fallen in zones under German control— evidently the soldiers felt it was up to each country to take care of its own dead.[15] The sentiment prevailed on both sides. As an Alsatian soldier named Dominique Richert remembered it, burying the dead was something his comrades did primarily for their fellow Germans; they were content to let the enemy dead lie there.[16] Similarly, one Dr. Leclerc, a professor at the Lille School of Medicine, recalled that "when a body fell into the hands of the enemy, they usually didn't bother to remove the dog tag hidden under the clothing."[17] And a lack of discipline on the part of the soldiers themselves sometimes complicated the task of identifying them: instead of following regulations and putting the tag firmly around their neck, many just wore it around their wrist or, worse, put it in a pocket or a wallet. For Philippe Fougerol, author of an information pamphlet for families, these soldiers were guilty of grave negligence that could lead to their going missing, unidentified, and to unrelieved anguish for their wives and relatives.[18] Faced with the extensiveness of the practice, in February 1915 Leclerc proposed a double identity-tag system, with one to be worn around the neck and one around the wrist.[19] In 1917, the initiative of Dr. A. M. Bosredon produced a new model: a tag worn around the wrist and made up of two parts, one connected to a chain (which would allow for identification in case of exhumation), the other detachable (which would provide the eidence to confirm a death).[20] This system worked well for the identification of bodies that were no longer physically recognizable. Still, it did nothing for the problem of the missing, beyond, perhaps, limiting their numbers by making the job of collecting tags easier for the men sent out to do so.

To make the job of identifying the dead simpler, and for instances when the battlefield remained inaccessible, the authorities could draw up a death notice even without a body. Two witnesses had to certify the death of the missing soldier. In theory, extra precautions would be taken in these circumstances. A distinction was made between certain death, which could be established by statements from two witnesses, and evidence for a death notice, which applied in cases where there was only one witness or where a body lacked a dog tag but had papers that could be used for identification. Such papers were not solid proof of identification, because, as the jurist Benjamin Duringer recalled, "On bodies we frequently found items of identification belonging to other individuals, some dead, some still living."[21] In practice, of course, the rules were not always followed.

Altogether, more than 300,000 men failed to answer roll call at the armistice. Soon enough, the term *missing* became a synonym for *dead*—which had not been the case before the war. Henceforth the term *beloved missing* evoked all the victims of the conflict, both those known to be dead and those assumed to be.[22] No distinction between the two groups was made on war memorials: a single homage honored the dead and the missing collectively. To separate them would be to sever the unity of their sacrifice. The commemorative plaque in the nave of the Church of Saint-Trophime in Arles was one of the very few to distinguish between the two groups. Dedicated in 1921, a time when no one held out any further hope, it nevertheless cited eighty-three dead and nineteen missing soldiers. If it was unthinkable by then to continue hoping for resurrections, perhaps the distinction can still be understood in terms of the distressing uniqueness of the missing veterans, as well as of the drama thrust upon their next of kin. Far from belittling them, it was an attempt to honor them more fully—a truly daring gesture, for in permanently establishing a dual status, it countered the possibility of any final mourning, of folding all the fallen heroes in a common shroud so that the nation might go on living. The Canadians also created a special homage for their missing: beginning in 1926, in the cemetery at Vimy—a theater of bloody combat in 1917—a tree was planted for every soldier lost. Today a forest covers the crest of Vimy.

In 1919, once the last prisoners had been repatriated from the internment camps, the time had come to acknowledge the deaths of the missing. Systematic searches for bodies in the immediate postwar period had brought their numbers down to 250,000, or some 17 percent of the total dead.[23] For the families, the hope of finding their loved ones' remains replaced the hope of seeing them come home from some enemy camp where they had been held in secret. But the slowness of the exhumations gave rise to bitter complaints from those who were enduring the pain of loss. Recalling Clemenceau's words on the duty of the living toward the dead, the bereft demanded that the searches be speeded up: "What are the appropriate agencies doing for soldiers killed or missing? . . . All battlefields were to be searched, they told us, 42,000 square kilometers of land to be thoroughly combed—promises so rich and consoling that we wanted to believe them."[24] The searches, which never went fast enough for those who were suffering, remained incomplete. Still, searches of the former war zone, divided into civilian sectors each under the command of an officer charged with exhumations and reburials, continued until 1939. When bodies with no identity tags or papers were exhumed, lists and descriptions of personal effects were all that families could go on to file a claim. It was not unusual to find announcements in the postwar press disclosing very meager information, such as one addressed to citizens of Aveyron by the committee for a monument at Notre-Dame de Lorette in Arras, following explorations on the battlefield at Artois: "The body of a French soldier has just been found in Wailly, some 1,500 meters southwest of the village.

He had a wallet with an envelope bearing a partially legible address with the name M. Du . . . , sent by Mme. Irénée Du. . . . The letter was sent from the Aveyron Department."[25]

For years after the war, the missing went on being identified and the dead soldiers, returned to their families, finally discharged. At the beginning of 1934, the bodies of sixty-seven soldiers were found in Pas-de-Calais alone.[26] A law of July 11, 1931, approved new funds—50 million francs for military cemeteries and another 10 million for the ongoing search for bodies.[27] The *Bulletin of the Union of Fathers and Mothers of Sons Who Have Died for Their Country,* which enumerated some 70,000 corpses found between 1919 and 1939, detailed the operations. First, a surface search enabled the recovery of thousands of bodies exposed by erosion. Next came deeper excavation in tunnels and trenches, using sounding rods. Teams operating at the front, which had by now been separated into fourteen sections, divided their labor by task in an effort to work more efficiently. The sounders, whose renowned skills made them capable of locating a body just by examining vegetation and its shades of color, were followed by the diggers, then the identifiers. To prevent callous farmers from ignoring any remains they might discover in their fields, property owners received a reward of ten francs for each corpse they turned in: "That is what the remains of a soldier are worth today," the *Bulletin* lamented.

But perhaps the most intriguing phenomenon was the spontaneous resurfacing of bodies. In a realistic assessment of the "earth and the dead," Maurice Barrès explored the theory that the soil is suffused and enriched by successive generations buried in it—a notion that gained in resonance following the war by virtue of the symbolism of soldiers disappearing into the very land they had died for: "In a phenomenon unexplained but verified a thousand times, evidently the war dead rise slowly from the depths where they are entombed when one day the earth, no longer needing them to defend or to nourish her, tosses them out, like the sea."[28]

Alas, the earth sometimes tossed them out too slowly for families to recover their bodies or pay last respects at their graves. Often the fathers and mothers were dead by the time it happened, and the dead soldier (now a civilian) died a second time, with no one left to mourn him. "It is infinitely sad," *L'Ancien Combattant de Paris* observed, "to see these unfortunate battle comrades emerge from oblivion only to return there forever."[29] At least the deaths of the aged parents finally put an end to the suffering born of their uncertainty.

Before receiving a grim visit from a mayor, a village policeman, or some other municipal employee announcing that a soldier had died or gone missing, families would already be in a state of anguish. Having had no letters for days, weeks, even months,[30] they would be expecting the worst. The wait for mail, which Stéphane Audoin-Rouzeau saw as "one of the most commonplace and least talked-about experiences of life back home,"[31] became a veritable torture. Anxious families would first blame the post office, then the military, which might be holding back letters from the front on the chance they contained information useful to the enemy; finally they would just hope for the next delivery—a stack of letters could all come at the same time. They watched for the mailman every morning. This tragic anticipation carried great emotional weight, which is why it found its way into literature and art. Henriette de Vismes describes the waiting in her novel *Letters without Answers,* in which a young woman who has not yet learned that her husband was killed in mid-August 1914 continues writing daily letters that he will never receive.[32] In the course of this one-way correspondence, which continues for seven weeks, the author plunges the reader (who knows from the outset that the husband is dead) into an introspection that the novel's interior monologue form further encourages. In an instance not drawn from fiction, Jane Catulle-Mendès received no news from her son, Primice, after a letter written on April 15, 1917. At first she refused to fret. As doubts began to overtake her, she worried, superstitiously, that in harboring them she was already casting her lot with the worst, running the risk of drawing disaster down onto her son. She continued to write every day, her letters more and more anguished, and she waited and watched for the mailman, eventually thinking of nothing else; she went so far as to imagine that her son had been captured—a fantasy that somehow soothed her.[33] Jane Catulle-Mendès was fortunate, at least, in the brevity of her uncertainty; she learned of her son's death after only fifteen days. Many other families whose men had disappeared saw their agony go on for weeks, even years.

The families of the missing had nothing to hold on to but a notice that their son or brother had disappeared on a certain date, in a certain place, presumably into either captivity or death.[34] The news plunged them into anxious uncertainty: Is he dead or is he alive? Is he rotting between the trenches? Has he been captured by the enemy? Days of prayer and waiting succeeded one another; the only hope was that a letter from a POW camp might diffuse their anxiety. Emile Joly, the mayor of Mende, in the department of Lozère, described the relief that finally came to those who had been fearing the worst on June 27, 1916—a month after an offensive that had left 750 soldiers missing from the 142nd Infantry, in which many local men served. Joly was convinced that death is easier to accept than disappearance; for him, the "natural and understandable" joy of families who had been reassured of their relatives' safety "only made the heartbreak and sorrow of those who had not received any news worse."[35] For those soldiers, in any case, the war was over. They were safe and sound and their next of kin solaced after suffering such a nightmare. But what about the others—those whose waiting went on and on, and who had no real reason to expect good news?

Yet families went on believing, refusing to accept any deaths that had not been confirmed, locked in a psychological torment that dragged on and on. Henriette Charasson wrote poems to her brother Cam, who had disappeared in September 1915 but whom she could not imagine dead, in an attempt to channel her heartache:

> *You are between Life and Death,*
> *Not yet in the black hole,*
> *Not yet in the night we know nothing about,*
> *But between Life and Death.*[36]

She stopped writing her poems in 1917. If they were mediocre artistically, they nevertheless carried great emotional weight for those who shared her suffering. Published in 1919 and reissued in 1929, they began with a poignant dedication from the sister to her brother: "To you who shared all my joys and my sorrows, these poems inspired by you, these poems of a happiness and a pain that you will not have known."

Madeleine Gaston-Charles, too, used poetry to speak of her sadness and her distress:

They left like all the others, gallant.
They left saying: "I will write often."
And since then, stoically, in our cruel pain,
We have feverishly awaited news.

They left. One day we heard no more about them!
And the months went by, marking time, sorrowful,
The women, hearts agonizing, torn apart,
Hope extinguishing the flickering flame.

What excruciating torture the ordinary evenings!
They are neither wounded nor captured.
Killed? Yet their names on dismal lists
Do not break through to the dense depths.

But if they were no more, there would be a tomb
Where we could weep for our fallen hero.
Yet no one knows, alas, where the body rests,
Or in what soil he sleeps his final sleep.

The earth that claims the bodily remains
Cannot hold back their splendor
And in remembering their glorious destiny,
Nothing reminds us that they were human!

No heavy stones weigh down on them,
They are in springtime, they are in light,
They are like a reflection of divinity.
Nothing is left of them in this world!

Nothing of what was brief, material, ephemeral,
Nothing but great glory . . . and great mystery!
They have taken off in sublime flight:
They are the missing, they are not the dead![37]

Caught in their drama, the relatives of the missing were hesitant to think of themselves as any more or less unhappy than those who knew for certain that their loved ones were dead, never to return. But the more reasonable among them tried to curb the futility of vain hope while still waiting for the end of the war to accept death—an acceptance made all the worse by the waiting. This was the thinking behind Jacques Rivière's plea that his wife, Isabelle, go ahead and mourn the death of her brother, Alain-Fournier: "Imagine how awful it would be to face death only at the war's end," he advised her in November 1914[38]—fruitlessly, for how can one be reasonable and still not want to believe? Jacques de Champfeu's family could not accept their fate, either, as a poem dedicated to his memory attests:

Your heart was still in the eternal silence.
Yet for all those months of waiting, we thought you were alive.
Having known this thrilling hope,
Is it not even worse, now, to have lost you?

You who disavowed those anonymous tombs,
We could not find your name among the dead,
Nor your last moments, nor your resting place—
We knew nothing of you but your sublime deeds.[39]

Unlike Alfred Drouin, who in his poem "To a Mother" saw her waiting as something "still sweet" compared to knowing that she would never again see her child,[40] Jacques de Champfeu's brother Philippe, in a posthumous letter written to the missing soldier on March 26, 1918, stressed the torment in the family's refusal to accept his death: "We had hoped that the bullets had spared you, and that, merely wounded, you had been taken in by the Germans, and cared for . . . ! And then time went by. The horrible silence went on unbroken. . . . It is so hard to believe in death when it touches you so closely!"[41]

The families did not just wait. Throughout the war they did their utmost, using every means in their power, to get information and to track down any trace of their lost sons and husbands. The newspapers overflowed with their desperate appeals. They ran lengthy supplications by tearful women. In a daily column called "Looking for . . . ," *La France de Bordeaux et du Sud-Ouest* ran dozens of appeals whose outcome was all too easy to guess: "To the attention of the gravely wounded or any other person returning from Germany who might have news of Private Firmin Bouffartigue . . . , gone missing the 20th of December: please contact Mme. Bouffartigue, 7 rue du Râteau, Bordeaux."[42] In July 1915, before the paper put an end to this depressing and futile column, wives were still hoping for the resurrection of husbands missing in combat since August 1914. On May 11, 1915, the mother of one Jean Julien L'Eglise sent her own desperate announcement to the paper; seven years later, she requested a photograph of Anthelme Mangin from Fenayrou in order to make certain that the Rodez amnesiac was not, by chance, the son for whom she had never given up hope.

The letter writers did not stop with the newspapers. They wrote the officers in the companies from which their men had gone missing; they wrote comrades; they wrote the priests in the towns nearest the places where their men had vanished, so that they might look for graves once the front lines had moved on; they wrote the local deputies[43] and especially the local mayors, who were besieged with questions and pleas to file requests with all the information services. The aforementioned mayor of Mende recalled the "difficult hours" when anguished families would come to him asking for help:

> I know nothing, and these desolate fathers, these weeping mothers, these despairing sisters, these hysterical wives believe that I do know something and that, out of pity for them, I don't want to tell them. At times like this the duties of a mayor are cruel to perform. One must console the

inconsolable; one must offer hope when one is convinced that all hope is lost.[44]

Most of the time, families took the initiative of contacting the appropriate organizations themselves. Various guides and brochures to assist them were published in 1915, such as one by Philippe Fougerol that supplied all the instructions for filing a request with the Ministry of War, even providing a sample.[45] Parisian city offices facilitated things by distributing a bulletin published by the Ministry of War's office of information. This office, housed in the École Militaire, was also the one that centralized all French requests for information and answered them, using lists of prisoners supplied to the Ministry of Foreign Affairs by Germany. Relatives of the missing could also call upon the prisoners' agency of the Red Cross, which transmitted requests to the organization's International Committee in Geneva, where a special agency, founded on August 15, 1914, received lists of prisoners from the warring nations—a requirement of both the Hague and Washington Conventions. In 1915, overwhelmed by the number of the missing and moved by the suffering of their families, Gustave Ador, the president of the International Committee, beseeched the warring heads of state to establish regular cease-fires to permit collection of the wounded and burial of the dead and to provide, as he put it, "relief from the unnecessary aggravation of the sufferings of this war."[46] To no avail. In the absence of humanitarian cease-fires, the problem of the missing remained, and organizations arose to deal with the pain of uncertainty.

The Association for the Search for the Missing, which had

its headquarters in Lyon, was one of the most important. It was attached to the French Red Cross's Agency for Prisoners of War, and it was headed by Augustin Radisson, administrator of the Society for Aid to Wounded Soldiers of the XIVth Military Region, a subgroup of the Red Cross. Most important, it had its own newspaper, *La Recherche des disparus,* a weekly with a pugnacious motto that ran in its first issue: "As long as the search has turned up nothing, we will pursue it with every means at our disposal."[47] The paper, sent free to all prefectures and subprefectures and to medical organizations, regimental depots, and refugee committees, became a rallying point for everyone involved in the search. All the names of soldiers repatriated from departments that had been invaded were published; so were private announcements from relatives or wives requesting news of missing soldiers. Beginning on January 30, 1916, *La Recherche des disparus* published photographs of these soldiers—a project with mostly meager results. After its seventy-third issue, on December 15, 1917, it suspended publication, citing a lack of funds and a shortage of paper, while promising that its searches would continue.[48]

News of the Soldier, though it had no newspaper of its own, was among the most active and well financed among other organizations, doubtless by virtue of its connections: it had been founded in October 1914 at the initiative of the Seine deputies, led by Denys Cochin, and was presided over by Henri Toussaint, a former attorney and magistrate at the Court of Appeals. The organization was recognized by decree on December 23, 1914, as one of the societies for aid to prisoners of war as dictated by the Hague Convention. Generous industrialists loaned offices, with initial funds coming from the Seine deputies, the city of Paris, the general council of the Seine region, various provincial general councils, and especially private donations. Provided with lists of prisoners in Germany by neutral correspondents, who did the same for the Germans, News of the Soldier strove to cross-check information by means of diverse lists of the wounded and the dead—from hospitals and ambulance services, from city halls, from information furnished by wounded soldiers who had been repatriated from Germany, and not least from direct investigations undertaken with the aid of mayors and priests in towns near the theater of war. At the end of December 1914, after an appeal by Denys Cochin to the Vatican, a pontifical decree ordered the cooperation of French and German bishops in searching for the missing and establishing chaplains in each camp to be expressly charged with correspondence between prisoners and their families. Periodically, lists of the missing were sent to Germany via neutral correspondents and posted in prisoner-of-war camps; in return, lists of missing German soldiers were posted in French POW camps, reciprocity being the best guarantee of mutual goodwill. In one year, if the president's activity report is to be believed,[49] some 60,000 requests came to the organization, and a little more than half received an answer. Yet few of the missing were located. Blame was apportioned variously between the "false clues found in misleading information from German organizations" and the "bad faith of the imperial authorities"—proof that cooperation had its limits. The Germans were suspected of using the missing as a psychological weapon. In Germany, the French were similarly suspected. In reality, News of the Soldier's failure can be explained by the lateness of the organization's involvement, which began only after investigations by the the Ministry of War's Office of Information and the Red Cross had turned up nothing. News of the Soldier was a last resort for those who went from office to office without ever accepting the unbearable truth of their loss, and was often useless, as the organization had the same lists as the official search agencies.

For those still unable to face the worst when all official means had been exhausted, there were other alternatives. Through the intercession of a parish priest or a bishop, relatives of the missing might contact the Pope himself—an option that, according to Francis Latour,[50] a large number of French citizens pursued. The Vatican received hundreds of letters daily and was soon overwhelmed. In an effort to deal with these pressing demands, it organized a special agency under the direction of one Father Reuter, whose more than 200 employees handled 16,000 requests for information from all over Europe between 1915 and the beginning of 1918.[51]

Though the Vatican had the lists of prisoners in every camp, it could no more assuage the grief of families than could the national organizations charged with finding the missing; but like them, it had no desire to extinguish all hope. Across the board, the standardized replies sought to spare those who received them. Thus Marie Laborde, who had been without news of her son since September 1914, received this cautious reply from the International Committee of the Red Cross on May 25, 1915:

We have not given up the search for the person you have asked about, but to our great regret we cannot furnish you with any positive information about Cpl. Pierre Laborde. All we can tell you is that, as of this date, your missing person does not figure on any of the official lists of prisoners, of the wounded, or of the dead. . . .[52]

The careful language notwithstanding, Cpl. Pierre Laborde was given up for lost. But his mother refused to accept the evidence and resorted to yet another avenue, which she found in the person of the king of Spain, writing to him along with a number of other desperate women. The royal intercession went through the embassy in Berlin, but it, too, failed, and it was only in 1925, when the corporal's body was found, that Marie could finally accept the death of her child and begin her mourning.

The months went by; the pointless measures multiplied; and hope faded that missing kin might be found alive. But without a body or even a death certificate, it was hard to be rational. The tension of prolonged uncertainty and the constant awareness of the drama pushed many relatives to the point of nervous collapse. "This implacable silence continues to gnaw at me, despite my best efforts,"[53] one father wrote to Dr. Adrien Granjux. Another echoed him: "The Christians' martyrdom in the Roman circuses seems like child's play to me. I'm being serious and literal. Compared to this five months' suffering, how bad could it be to suffer for fifteen or twenty minutes?"[54] Their health deteriorated. Some declined so badly that they drew the attention of mental-health specialists. As early as March 1915, the question preoccupied Granjux, who analyzed their descent into neurasthenia and pathological melancholy—always, like his colleagues, keeping in mind the notion of predisposition—in a letter to the Society of Legal Medicine. The situation, he observed, was all the more serious because "in their milieu they were not considered ill and did not consult a neurologist or a psychiatrist." One Dr. Antheaume agreed that melancholic anxiety with suicidal tendencies was a state of mind shared by many relatives of the missing.

Psychologically debilitated, families deprived of mourning were easy prey for all kinds of scams, and the more so because they were ready to follow any lead—even the most irrational. Swindlers profited from their distress, extorting money in exchange for information promised by a supposed information network with agents in Germany. On September 22, 1915, *Le Bulletin des réfugiés du Nord* denounced one such con man plying his schemes under cover of a fictitious organization called the Help for Families.[55] When any of these criminals was arrested—for example, a woman tried by court-martial in the XVIIIth Military Region at the beginning of 1915, whose deeds were reported by *La France de Bordeaux et du Sud-Ouest*—the sentence was usually severe and widely approved.

The most characteristic manifestation of mental distress, however, was not in the swindles reported but, rather, in resorting to the irrational—to spiritualism. Mediums, unlike pastors, were quite willing to try to establish direct contact with the dead. With no news of Joseph Foulquier, declared missing on March 18 , 1915, at Mesnil-les-Hurlus, his family contacted a clairvoyant for reassurance. "Last night I went to find a woman like the one Mama wanted to go see," his sister wrote. "She told me that Joseph wasn't dead but that he had been wounded, and that in a few days we would get news that would make the whole family happy. Oh, if that were true, if he could come back—that's the important thing."[56] Turning to magic to pierce the wall of silence may be understandable, but once the war was over it could become pathological—as in the case of the widow who in 1921 was still running from hypnotist to fortune-teller, trying to locate her husband. He had fallen in the second battle of the Marne, in 1918, and, because she could not bring herself to believe that he was dead, she was regarded as "half-mad."[57] In truth, France was full of the half-mad who could not bring themselves to mourn.

As Michel Hanus has noted, *mourning* is a term with multiple meanings: the state that follows the loss of a loved one; the social behaviors, individual and collective, called for in honoring the dead; and, finally, the psychic work that allows one to accept the reality of the loss.[58] This astonishingly complex and sad behavior fascinated Freud, who attempted to analyze it from an ethnographic viewpoint in 1912, in *Totem and Taboo*,[59] then went deeper with *Thoughts for the Times on War and Death*[60] and *Mourning and Melancholy*,[61] both written in 1915, at the very moment when, with three sons on the front lines, he was dreading, and attempting to prepare himself for, their deaths.[62] For him, the enigmatic, ineffable pain of mourning arose from a narcissistic investment—"the lost person experienced as a part of oneself"[63]—which explained the state of shock during the first moments of mourning, when death is not yet acknowledged because it is intolerable, unacceptable. When the mayor of Mende learned of the death of his son, on November 16, 1917, he rejected and denied the horrible news: "But it's crazy to believe it! No, it's not possible. It's not true! My child! My Paul!"[64] But facts cannot long be denied. In making the effort, in his unhappiness, to know "the atrocious truth" rather than live with "the maddening uncertainty,"[65] the mayor of Mende was already moving in the direction of acceptance.

The process described by psychoanalysts, which moves from denial of death to a slow emotional disassociation from the lost person, had no analogue in the families of the missing. How could they accept the reality of death when there were no body and no witnesses, not even an official notice? Their efforts to go on believing, in spite of everything, that their loved ones were alive, their repeated requests for information from the Ministry of War, the Red Cross, or the Vatican even though the prisoner lists—and, therefore, the responses— were everywhere the same, obviously betokened a denial of the pain of mourning. Being missing was, in effect, an undefined social state that rendered unusable all the rituals and practices that society has developed to deal with such sadness. Families could not wear black. They might be pitied but could not partake of the honor attached to the relatives of anyone who had "died for his country." A woman could continue receiving the mobilization allotment but not a widow's pension. Inheritance could not be established. Without certainty, time was frozen and peace of mind out of reach. Were those who had certainty, who had gravesides at which to meditate, aware of their "luck," aware that not everyone was so blessed? Germaine Franchemont's prayer for her grandson, dead at the Somme in 1916, emphasized the importance of knowing the circumstances of the death and of having the body in order to assuage one's pain. She even saw in these elements the work of grace:

> Because you allowed us to know the precise details
> Of his last moments
> And to know that he did not suffer,
> I thank you, Lord.

> Because he fell in French territory,
> Because we could find his tomb
> And wash the sacred earth with our tears that he washed
> with his blood,
> I thank you, Lord.[66]

During the conflict, Henri Toussaint, the president of News of the Soldier, noted the relief that swept over relatives of the missing when he told them that a body had finally been recovered. He concluded that the ordeal of waiting is unlike any other.[67] An enamel plaque placed on the tomb of a "beloved husband" after the war bears witness to this need for a body and a fixed place for the work of mourning: a woman who wept for her lost love there insisted that the only consolation left her was "to kneel on that icy stone."[68]

Once every avenue had been explored and the passing months left no further hope, once the promises held out by charlatans, clairvoyants, hypnotists, and fortune-tellers had failed, irrationality and rumors took over: the missing were still alive but held in secret by the Germans, in camps unknown either to the Red Cross or neutral nations. A hope like that was far from ridiculous if it was the final one, and it came to seem possible simply by being expressed. The names of certain prisoners were deliberately being removed from the lists given to the Ministry of Foreign Affairs, to the Vatican, and to the International Committee of the Red Cross, and the prisoners were being prevented from writing—that was all there was to it! Starting in January 1915, the daily *Le Télégramme* set out to calm its readers' worries by explaining the real reason for the absence of news: families who received a notice from the military authority that a soldier had gone missing should not lose heart, because the count of the wounded and the dead was performed with "extreme care. . . . If a soldier was declared missing, this meant that he figured neither among the former nor among the latter." In other words, "the husband or the son was in good health but a prisoner of the enemy." The callous withholding of information as practiced by the Germans, *Le Télégramme* continued, was the sole reason for the silence.[69] The following March, Granjux put a scientific stamp on the rumor of a "secret camp," stating in a report on the psychological state of the relatives of the missing to the Society of Legal Medicine:

Today most of the "missing" are part of a new category: the wounded soldiers or prisoners for whom the Germans—in a true refinement of cruelty—have removed any possibility of sending news to their relatives. This category . . . consists principally of the wounded soldiers and prisoners from the beginning of the war, whose relatives, as a consequence, have been without news of their loved ones' fate for seven long months.[70]

To put an end to this base "psychological blockade," the eminent specialist proposed preventing German prisoners from writing to their own relatives, in a just response to "Kraut cynicism": "Thus we might perhaps create an opportunity for some improvement in the inhumane system the French are subject to in Germany."[71]

In other words, there were no "missing." German callousness explained them away. In August 1915, the *Bulletin des réfugiés du Nord* offered a report, based on the revelations of a nurse who had returned from German captivity, that should interest "all those who have been without news from those considered missing." Contingents of French prisoners, the article declared, were being used clandestinely to dig German trenches and labor in German military works:

Such men were considered dead by the Berlin government, which reported nothing about them and did not make their whereabouts known.

Thus many of those who have spent months waiting for

letters from sons or husbands known to have been only slightly wounded and taken prisoner but who, nevertheless, have shown no sign of life, will learn after the war that their sons and husbands have worked for the Germans for many months amid Belgian and French crews.

This news should give hope to many French men and women who have had no certainty about any possible misfortunes. One must not exaggerate the hope, but it isn't futile.[72]

A few days later, the *Bulletin* reiterated its credo: "Mothers, wives, children plunged into darkness after the disappearance of a son, a husband, or a father: Do not despair. Those you weep for may be imprisoned in Germany."[73] Under the circumstances, and even with no official voice confirming the myth of secret camps, how not to believe it? How not to hope for the return of the missing at the end of the war? "You will return when the great victory greets the day," wrote Henriette Charasson to her missing brother.[74] "It seems I shall always wait for you, month after month, all my life long. With white hair I hope to see you reappear; it is only sometimes, at certain moments, that I can believe you are dead."[75] Similarly, Madeleine Pambrun, in her diary, could not accept the idea that her brother, Henry, was really dead:

It's strange—I always hold out hope. It seems as if an extraordinary thing had happened and that this word *missing* doesn't mean: *death.* . . . Why shouldn't we be among the many families who have had no news for two or three years because the missing were kept from writing? It's a mad hope, maybe, but it has never left me.[76]

After November 11, 1918, she eagerly awaited the return of the prisoners who might bring miraculous surprises back with them. But by the early months of 1919 she knew that the "madness of hope" had frayed and that the missing were never going to return.

The shock was terrible for everyone who had placed hope in the idea of secret German camps. They had soothed themselves with illusions, and the dream that had kept them going was now abruptly shattered. When they could no longer deny death, the relatives of the missing switched to another illusion: their loved ones had been taken as prisoners to Germany and then executed in the deepest silence. Gathering at Trocadéro on March 27, 1919, under the auspices of the National Federation of the Search for the Missing, they clamored for vengeance. Facing a crowd of five thousand distraught people, Deputy Aristide Prat, the president of the Union of Families of the Missing—an association created in 1917 with the support of the president of France, the minister of foreign affairs, and the minister of war—launched a blistering attack against an underhanded Germany that had constantly, consciously lied. Citing soldiers who had been kept from writing and then, when they were thought dead, miraculously returned home, he denounced the bad-faith "cooperation" of the Germans, with their phony prisoner lists. "What did they do with our prisoners? What did they do with three hundred thousand men?" he thundered, before proceeding to threats:

> The time has passed when, practically trembling, we asked them to help, to support us. Here now is what we are asking for, what we are demanding.
>
> We want special commissions charged with going to Germany with full powers to investigate for themselves, in the former camps, in the fortresses, the mines, the caverns, the forests, everywhere, for traces of our prisoners. . . .
>
> None of you, ladies and gentlemen, will have complete satisfaction, none of you will have real peace until the day when these searches end, when we will be able to say to Germany: Now, atone for what you have done![77]

At the end of his heavily applauded speech, the family members got a chance to speak out even more vehemently:

> We are the families the Germans have tortured, the families who, because of them, have suffered everything that it is humanly possible to suffer. Well, now we demand vengeance!
>
> [*Cries of "Bravo!"*]
>
> . . . Our voices must be heard all the way to the peace conference. . . . We demand sanctions and reparations.[78]

In the course of the speeches, each more passionate than the one before, criticism that was at first directed unanimously against Germany eventually turned against the French government. It was accused of inaction, of weakness in the face of a defeated enemy, of insufficient urgency in its search for bodies on the former battlefields. Aristide Prat faithfully relayed these criticisms to the Chamber of Deputies. On June 19, 1919, he faced the minister of war. Prat acknowledged that, of the three hundred thousand missing, a good half still lay in the soil where they had died. But he demanded to know what happened to the rest—those who had been taken prisoner and then had never written and never returned. Recalling that the Germans had given their word of honor to cooperate in the search for the missing during the war as long as the French did the same, he was interrupted by a colleague: "Word of honor doesn't exist for the Krauts."[79] The undersecretary of state for the Ministry of War offered a dispassionate explanation: the missing, estimated at 314,000, were composed mainly of soldiers buried by the French or the Germans without having been identified. Then there was the category of soldiers pulverized by the explosion of shrapnel or mines, lost between the trenches, and for whom searches had yet to be carried out. Finally, a third category—perhaps a little more than two hundred individuals—consisted of surviving soldiers who, "for various reasons," did not wish to return, out of fear of prosecution for desertion, for example.

His explanation was correct. But it could neither convince nor satisfy people obsessed with finding parties to blame for their misery. On July 5, the government finally sent a team of military investigators to Germany to satisfy them; it turned up nothing. By that time, all requests for information addressed to the information office of the Ministry of War were receiving the same reply: "Any soldier declared missing who has not by now reappeared must be considered deceased. In fact, all war prisoners have been repatriated or are on lists of those placed in known German health facilities."[80] Families rebelled, refusing to accept this answer. On July 5, some of them presented a final petition to Clemenceau, the president of the Council, pleading that he act with force and speed to find "the missing, the hidden war martyrs whom the indifferent presume dead but whom we, in our hearts, as mothers and wives, and encouraged by numerous irrefutable statements, hope are still alive, at least some of them, in jails or penal colonies, in Germany or elsewhere."[81] It received no response. On July 17, the Ministry of War closed its family information service, which no longer served any function. Finally, at the end of August 1919, the *Bulletin de l'Union des familles de disparus* itself ceased to appear, ostensibly because of its high cost but in reality because the organization no longer had any reason to exist. The struggle had ended because hope was dead.

That was why the case of Anthelme Mangin, the living unknown soldier, attracted the attention and reawakened the hope of everyone whose son, husband, or brother he might be.

"Honor to the dead!" declaimed Georges Clemenceau to the Chamber of Deputies on Armistice Day, November 11, 1918; they "achieved this victory for us!"[82] With the war over, the country, orphaned by its 1,400,000 dead and missing, acknowledged the sacrifice and rendered homage to the heroes who had died for their country by engraving their names on monument stones in every city and town in France. The dead were always a part of the celebrations. In Toulouse, for the announcement of the armistice, the crowd on streets paved in the three colors of the French flag surged spontaneously to the Terre-Cabade cemetery, making it a place of fellowship for a people worn down by the four-year ordeal.[83] In Paris, on July 13, 1919, the night before Bastille Day—which was also a victory celebration—a cenotaph was placed under the Arc de Triomphe with the inscription "To those who died for their country." Thus were the dead gathered there symbolically, thereby beginning a day of transformation for their surviving comrades, led by a thousand wounded veterans—the amputated, the blinded, the disfigured.[84] "The dead, all the glorious and wretched dead of the victory, had to be the first to pass under the Arc de Triomphe. And that is what happened,"[85] Maurice Prax exulted in *Le Petit Parisien*.

The rituals Patrick Cabanel called "the sacrament of November 11"[86]—homage to the dead, mourning by the living, the nation crucified and brought back to life—could not then be observed just once, but had to rise, constant and perpetual, to the drama. It was for this reason that on September 12, 1919, a group of eighty-eight deputies, led by André Maginot and Maurice Maunoury, requested that an "obscure soldier," a hero all the more anonymous because his identity had been lost in the firestorm, be transferred to the Panthéon. This initiative crowned a process begun during the French Revolution, the defining era of national and democratic wars. It was no longer enough to erect a monument to victorious military leaders; now it was necessary to honor the glory of anonymous citizen-soldiers. In 1871, the prince of Joinville, son of

Louis-Philippe, first put forward this idea, proposing that the Vendôme column, which the Communards had destroyed, be reconstructed with the statue of a simple soldier taking the place of Napoléon.[87] On November 20, 1916, in the midst of the war, the president of an organization called French Memory was among the first to proffer the idea of burying an unknown soldier in the Panthéon,[88] an idea taken up by the members of Parliament in 1919. Yet the deputies' proposal did not seek merely to give the country a national altar where the remains of a martyr would symbolize the sacrifice of all; it sought to deal as well with the suffering families of the missing, by giving them a body they could imagine belonged to them. Once again, the French were not all equal in their mourning. Those who could not kneel down and weep over a grave, who did not know where or when their loved ones had died—those people knew the importance of a "space for solitude" that, as the journalist Séverine noted, would ease the pain of the survivors.[89] Cemeteries would set aside a special place for the missing, where their relatives could come "to pay unofficial tribute"; families excluded from mourning could thus practice the rituals of funerary honor.[90] It was also to meet this need for solidarity with suffering families that the law of September 12, 1919, proposing the memorial, sought to "bring glory to those disinherited from death":

In future centuries, the memorial will represent the citizen fallen for his country! Next to Rouget de Lisle, who first sang the *Marseillaise*, a child of France will embody it, and families of the missing will take pride in visiting a site that will give them the sensation of visiting the tomb of those they weep for.[91]

This "official nameless body"[92] would provide the means of exalting not only the sacred body of a nation that had undergone its own Passion but also the earthly bodies of those who had disappeared into the fire. If this second dimension of the Unknown Soldier gradually faded with the generation of the war, it was vividly present for contemporaries. *Le Matin* put it precisely: although the Unknown Soldier "represents the generation of sacrifice," he was also, and especially, "the son of all the mothers who did not recover their sons."[93] The instructions André Maginot gave regarding the choice of the body left no doubt about the deference to soldiers lost on the battlefield and never identified: "For the body that will be moved to the Panthéon, our main concern is to assure the most complete anonymity, so that families who suffered the misfortune of losing one of their own in the war, eternally unidentified, can always imagine that their dearly beloved is the very object of this supreme tribute."[94] The families in question were not mistaken in believing that a national honor was being bestowed upon their kin.

The ceremony marking the choice of the Unknown Soldier in the fort at Verdun was designed to comfort them: each time an anonymous casket crossed the threshold of the room where Private Thin held the bouquet of flowers that would designate the one who would represent the sacrifice of all, Officer Lespinasse commanded: "In the name of all unknown soldiers on all battlefields, let the drums roll"—and they rolled for the dead. Finally, when the chosen coffin emerged from the fort, women in black pressed around to touch it, and one made her way close enough to kiss the wood. "All mothers who do not know where their children lie can believe, like this one, that their own has received the highest honors,"[95] a general observed. And when the archbishop of Paris was invited to bless the body during the ceremony of November 11, 1920, even though the Unknown Soldier and his family might easily have been Protestant, or Jewish, or atheist, no argument was raised, this corpse of one nameless soldier having taken on the nature of a collective body. A poem by Rabbi Honel Mess bore witness:

> *O France, my beloved France,*
> *Forever may you be blessed*
> *For erasing the sorrow*
> *That was breaking our heart!*
> *Today every wife, every sister, every mother,*
> *Exalting the career of her beloved "missing person,"*
> *Can proudly say, without illusion:*
> *It must certainly be he who is entering the Panthéon!*
> *O veteran, take your place*
> *There in the glorious monument.*
> *Soldiers of your kind*
> *Deserve the granite resting spot of a giant!*[96]

Thus were the families of the missing, with neither body, nor ritual, nor graveside, reintegrated into the community of mourning; and it was via their mourning and their particular tragedy that the polemics ended in unanimity. On November 13, 1920, *L'Œuvre* announced in its columns that a Senegalese soldier had been exhumed at Verdun but not included for consideration as the Unknown Soldier. The paper asked: "Wasn't he a soldier just like the others?"[97] Blaise Diagne, the deputy from Senegal, spoke out against the decision; but his anger was quelled by the necessary anonymity of the Unknown Soldier, and by the sense that the French needed to recognize in him their lost child.

Similarly, uproar surrounding the debate over where to bury the Unknown Soldier quieted before the suffering of the families. Until the beginning of November 1920, the Panthéon had the upper hand as the site for the memorial, but in the end it was rejected. For the political right, which had become the majority in the 1919 elections, the Panthéon was too tied to the left; as Leon Daudet pointed out, they were running the risk of seeing the glorious Frenchman who died to save his country right next to that Dreyfus supporter Émile Zola, who certainly didn't figure in the conservatives' pantheon.[98] The November 8, 1920, session of the Chamber of Deputies was devoted entirely to this debate, and Deputy Gaston Vidal was one of the few to affirm that "the place is of little importance; what is important is the gesture, only the gesture."[99] The issue became a matter of public debate, and to put it to rest the government backed off from its original choice of the Panthéon and chose the Arc de Triomphe, concurring with the editorial views of several newspapers. *L'Intransigeant,* led by its director, Leon Bailby, and Gabriel Boissy, was at the heart of the press campaign claiming this very highest honor for the unknown citizen-soldier. For Boissy, a veteran, nothing could be too glorious. Traumatized by the fear of going missing during the conflict, he had dedicated his first postwar book to those comrades of his who were never found: "To my dearest friends, whose bodies hover there, in the bloody sod, beneath the eucharistic crown of iron thorns."[100] In 1915, wounded and convalescing, he described the terror of going missing, a terror that had not ceased to haunt him and that he sought to put an end to by making himself the voice of the lost soldiers:

> I dream of the dead that we left back there, half-buried. Will I end up the same way? Death is acceptable, certainly, but this oblivion, this abandonment, this anonymity? . . . My whole person rebels against this sacrifice to the unknown, which goes far beyond the unknown that is death. . . .
>
> Yes, I accept death, but I hope for witnesses. Yet here we disappear among a multitude of events, among thousands of men pulverized by the force of shrapnel. Do we have to add abnegation to humility?[101]

The main argument put forward by those who preferred the Arc de Triomphe was that the Unknown Soldier was not a great man on the order of those heroes buried in the Panthéon and, for that reason, belonged elsewhere. "Reserve a place for him in a crypt! Next to whom?" *Le Matin* demanded. "Does his glory have anything in common with that of the others?"[102] He had to be by himself, at the summit of the triumphal avenue, outshining with his anonymous presence, symbol of the nation's sacrifice, all those military leaders whose names are engraved in the stones of the monument. Carrying on the nation's past victories, he would mark a kind of end to them as well, because his tomb would forever seal off the passage under the arch. No one would march beneath it any longer—the price of reaping laurels had been too high, and the public wanted to believe that this had really been the war to end all wars.

The socialists were the most vehement in rejecting the idea of the Arc de Triomphe, making their case as passionately as they had when they had rejected the idea of burying an unknown soldier in the first place. They saw in this choice of site an honor for the military, as well as a final trick played on a proletarian sent off to be butchered, "an anonymous victim immolated for profane profiteering,"[103] whose corpse would never be decommissioned but instead would be forever loaded with militaristic honors. Faced with the fervor of the public, however, they suppressed their disapproval and decided that the body of an unknown soldier was worthy of all honors— which allowed them to approve the ceremony. An article in *Le Populaire* on November 11, 1922, affirmed this reversal: the "mobilization of the living dead" was still a problem, but the corpse was given back his civilian status—"The unknown of l'Etoile is not a soldier, he is only a man, a man who loved life." He had became "a symbol of pain, of mourning, of cold, somber death."[104] Thus solidarity was achieved around the mourning of those gone missing through one unknown body and a funerary ceremony that was more than merely patriotic. For, finally, what did these debates matter to the father of a lost son who would build a model of the Arc de Triomphe to hold the portrait of his child?[105] His child had been properly honored.

But the existence of other unknown soldiers, still alive, presented a difficulty, even if they had been removed from society. Their portraits, appearing in the newspapers in 1922, revived the anguish that had been channeled into the cult of the Unknown Soldier and suddenly challenged its success. For the symbol to have any meaning—for the symbolic body and the earthly body to be one—there had to be a single, unique Unknown Soldier. Shortly after the grand ceremony at the Arc de Triomphe, *Le Courrier de l'Aveyron* had proposed having Unknown Soldiers in every city in France for the benefit of parents, wives, orphans, and fiancées who could visit the tombs—an idea that was received with some enthusiasm.[106] But the proposal was ferociously attacked by veterans, who rose up in anger when they learned that local governments were granting these honors in perpetuity to unidentified soldiers. In January 1921, the members of the Le Mans chapter of the National Veterans Union adopted a resolution: "The tribute rendered in Paris last November 11 by all of France to the French soldier whose body lies under the Arc de Triomphe must, to conserve the grandeur of its meaning and the beauty of its symbolism, remain unique."[107] The idea of burying an unknown veteran from the North African contingent of the French army in Marseille also faltered.[108] The Arc de Triomphe had become the undisputed center of national commemoration for the Great War. Every trip to Paris had to be punctuated by a visit there, and twice a week municipal employees had to remove the faded flowers piled up on the tomb. On November evenings, one journalist reported, mourning relatives were even more numerous than usual:

> A man or a woman whose son did not return from the war would go to place flowers and pay homage under the Arc de Triomphe, and without knowing one another, other fathers and mothers of missing soldiers could exchange greetings and say:
> "Maybe he's *your* son!"
> "Maybe he's *yours!*"[109]

In February 1922, when Anthelme Mangin's photograph appeared, three hundred thousand families were suddenly faced with the same possibility.

Chapter Three

The Return of Colonel Chabert

On February 3, 1935, *Le Journal des mutilés et combattants* compared Anthelme Mangin to a character out of a novel, noting that reality often imitates fiction: "It is not only in the imagination of novelists that individuals exist who are living and dead at the same time, veritable human shipwrecks without names or personalities, at the margins of society."[1] Even earlier, *Le Petit journal,* considering the mystery of Mangin's identity, had exclaimed, "What a beautiful subject for a novel!"[2] In fact, the Rodez amnesiac was the quintessence of literary myth, a myth that created him as much as he nourished it.

The postwar passion for commemoration brought the dead into the very heart of cities. With these memorials, the living avowed that they would never forget the dead, that they would forever remain in their debt. Given such feelings, it is easy to understand how traumatizing readers found the conclusion Roland Dorgelès drew in *Les Croix de bois,* insisting on what no one wanted to hear: "It's true, we will forget. Oh! I know, it's hateful, it's cruel, but why get incensed—it's human. . . . The veils of mourning will fall like dead leaves. The image of the lost soldier will fade slowly from the hearts of those who loved him so much. And the dead will die a second time."[3] But his contemporaries refused to believe that it was possible to forget the heroes. And so they nourished a deep guilt born of the distance between their daily preoccupations— life went on—and the dejection and reflection, individual and collective, that death called for.

The guilt of surviving, of continuing to enjoy life when someone else has disappeared, of forgetting, little by little, the one who died, has a significant place in literature, in particular via the theme of the missing person's return. The scholar Jay Winter has described it this way: A man is believed dead; time passes; and then his sudden reappearance creates a huge shock, a living reproach to a world that has accustomed itself to his death and gotten along well without him, a world that has forgotten him so thoroughly that when he comes back he no longer has a place in it.[4] Such is the plot of Balzac's 1832 novel *Colonel Chabert.* The title character is left for dead on the battlefield at Eylau in 1807. His wife quickly marries Count Ferraud. Chabert's unexpected return places her new fortune at risk. She uses her charm to ward off scandal; and Chabert, disgusted, resigns himself to poverty and anonymity in a world that rejects him.

The theme of Balzac's novel was popular between 1914 and 1918, appearing again and again, the plot always intact:

a soldier disappears in battle; an official notice is received; time passes; his wife remarries; and all of a sudden there he is, having escaped from Germany, where he was held prisoner— a shocking return from the dead. The story might take the form of an absurd or grotesque vaudeville, with tears hiding behind laughter, as in a short story that appeared in *Le Siècle*, in which a prisoner thought dead escapes and returns to his home, now occupied by another man. The soldier works out an arrangement: on military leaves, he will enjoy conjugal rights with his wife; when he is away, she will be entrusted to his capable replacement.[5] There is a happy ending, too, in a vulgar little play called *Chez vous, chez moi* (*Your Place, My Place*), in which a soldier declared dead escapes from Germany to find the apartment of his mistress abandoned; she has not waited for him. But its new tenant is charming, he falls in love with her, and a rapid marriage makes up for the insult of having been forgotten.[6]

Barreyre and Morin's drama *Leur ami* (*Their Friend*) is more serious. It honors the memory of the dead by putting onstage a faithful, loving wife who does not believe the notice of her husband's death and consequently holds the advances of other suitors at bay, insisting that her husband will return: "Some premonitions are never wrong! My husband is living, I feel it, I am sure of it."[7] And three years after the news of his death, the husband, who has been held prisoner and prevented from writing her, shows up at home, and the good wife, Marie, concludes by addressing the audience directly: "You see, one must believe in premonitions."[8] The unexpected resurrection and the recovered happiness convey a larger refusal to accept the death of soldiers.

In spite of everything, of course, life did go on, and the men who came back did not always find their homes just as they had left them. That seems to be the theme of *Le Retour*, a three-act play by Pierre Berch. The literary work closest to the outlines of Balzac's novel, it concerns a woman who, having received notice of her husband's death, remarries and bears a child. But Jacques, Jane's first husband, is not dead, and after three years of hiding in enemy territory he returns and forcefully demands his rightful place. When Jane refuses to abandon the man who has made her a mother, Jacques tries to kill her—then realizes that he is in the wrong and leaves forever.[9] Berch probably got his inspiration from an article in *La Française* of July 1916, about just such a tangled tragedy of the war:

> At the very beginning of the war, a woman receives notice of her husband's death on the battlefield.
>
> Despair, no doubt, but also prompt consolation, because as soon as legally possible she remarries. . . .
>
> A child is born to this legal and consecrated union in 1916. But to the war widow's surprise, her first husband turns up. He had been a prisoner and unable to send news until then.
>
> So the woman is a bigamist! And the child, what is he—legitimate, adulterous offspring, bastard? Will the mother have the right to choose between her two husbands? If the first resumes his role in the conjugal home, what will the

child be to him? Is an amicable arrangement possible? All difficult questions to answer![10]

At this point there was so much denial of death that literature was not enough to soothe the anxieties of the day—contemporaries were busy piling up incredible stories of soldiers returning after they had been declared dead. Blame was laid on the mistakes of the military information offices, on the German refusal to let prisoners in "special" camps communicate, and on all but unbelievable circumstances, as in the story about the Breton whose arm was found on the battlefield, his wrist bearing the regulation identity tag; the death certificate was issued and his wife remarried, only to learn the awkward truth soon afterward.[11] Another story, drawn from the testimony of a Red Cross nurse and recounted by Paul Masson in his law thesis, involved a wounded Frenchman in a hospital near Lille who was put in bed with a card indicating his identity. When the enemy arrived, he had to relinquish his place to a severely wounded German, who died shortly afterward, just as the French were retaking the territory. A death certificate was drawn up using the information on the card, even while the soldier in question, taken captive by the Germans, was still living.[12]

The end of the conflict and the beginning of the prisoners' return gave new vigor to accounts of this kind. Georges Duhamel recorded one of these improbable stories of resurrection in his *Entretiens dans le tumulte* (*Conversations Amid the Turmoil*):

A good woman lost her husband in 1914, right at the begin-
ning of the war. He was declared missing in the month of
September, and his utter silence verified the putative death.
After waiting for nearly four years, the woman remarried. . . .

One morning the woman was informed that her first
husband had just arrived in London in a mixed group of
repatriated prisoners. She also learned that the unfortunate
man had had both his arms amputated and that he hadn't
been able to send word for four years because he'd been held
in a special camp, owing to his insubordination.[13]

On December 3, 1918, *Le Matin* saluted a similar return;
the missing man had also been interned in a special camp, unable to communicate with his family.[14] In February 1919, the
Canard dieppois reported the homecoming reactions of prisoners thought definitely dead: these now unwanted men could
cause havoc if they "became indignant" and "lashed out," but
for the most part they resigned themselves to their fate and
abandoned "the ex-conjugal home."[15] There were not many
such stories of unhoped-for returns, but the alacrity with
which they were reported underlined a fundamental need to
believe that the missing were alive, a refusal to accept their
deaths. And, of course, as paradoxical as it might seem, there
was also fear of those who would reappear to reclaim their
roles in a society that no longer needed them. In some ways,
the stories were suspect, inasmuch as they ignored the law (the
legal period before a widow could remarry being only ten
months), they readily accepted the notion that a prisoner

might leave his family without news for three years, and they swallowed whole the myth of the "secret camps" where the Germans, in their effort to demoralize the French public, were holding prisoners incommunicado and hiding their identity from the French Ministry of Foreign Affairs, the International Red Cross, the king of Spain, and the Pope.[16] Finally, in each case, the wife of the missing man had decided to remarry and remake her life: the stories were suspiciously similar. But if they were false, the anguish they expressed was far from false.

The wives' good faith was not in doubt. Officially widows, they had garbed themselves in mourning, waited the prescribed period, and only then had said yes to other men. Their weddings were conventional ceremonies in city halls and in churches. All the same, the women were considered suspect and often guilty—guilty of not having honored for far longer the memory of a hero, of having too easily forgotten him. The Breton writer Charles Le Goffic scornfully called them "widows in a hurry,"[17] and with Magistrate Henri Robert, sought to prohibit the remarriage of widows for the duration of the war.

But the world of the dead is not that of the living, and the delicate situation of the wives of the missing—half-dead, half-alive men whose death certificates could not be issued—preoccupied civil society. These were widows who had no legal rights to inheritance, who could not remarry, and who could not have children fathered by other partners recognized as legitimate. In 1916, Jean Callier, in his law thesis, favored the idea of new marriages for wives of the missing with the goal of "facilitating repopulation."[18] In 1922, his colleague Jacques Humblot

also defended second marriages for the wives of dead or missing soldiers—in addition to satisfying the need for love and
tenderness, they would act as guarantors of morality by preventing the "disorder and debauchery" of cohabitation and
frivolous liaisons that the partnerless sought out to "satisfy
their passion."[19] A law passed by the Chamber of Deputies on
March 31, 1919, permitting remarried women to retain the
legal benefits of their first marriages elicited violent criticism.
Wasn't it unseemly to allow remarried widows the advantage
of income "won at the cost of blood" by deceased soldiers?[20]
But it was also clear that the law that existed before the war,
conceived for a few rare cases,[21] was not adequate to the cases
of tens of thousands of women "tied, often very young, to a
marriage that no longer existed."[22] On December 3, 1915, the
Civil Legislation Committee of the Chamber of Deputies had
expanded the law of June 8, 1893, relating to sailors lost at
sea, which authorized tribunals to declare a death officially
"when there existed proof or serious, precise, or cumulative
presumption furnished by witnesses."[23] But when there were
no witnesses, as were the majority of the wartime cases? A law
enacted on June 24, 1919, finally delivered the living from
their phantom mates by converting absence into death, on the
condition that two years had passed since the disappearance.
If the husband reappeared, the new marriage would be an-
nulled, but any children born of the union would be considered legitimate and would retain their inheritance rights as well
as all obligations related to their legitimacy.[24] La Vie parisienne
found fault with the law, arguing that the choice in such cases
should belong to the wife.

The adaptation of existing law to new situations created by the war was inevitable. But legal solutions to the problems of the missing could not address the questions of doubt and the feelings of guilt. As one journalist demanded, "Won't there remain a secret anguish in the hearts of those who obtain a ruling of freedom from the court?"[25]

The anguish really extended to all of civil society, not just the widows onto whom this collective guilt was imposed. Disappointed expectations in relation to the war, doubts regarding the meaning of sacrifice, feelings of unworthiness for continuing to live almost normal lives—these sore spots gave rise to fear that a kind of supreme soldier would appear, accusing and punishing. The fear was that much stronger because the undefined state of the missing, somewhere between life and death, reawakened ancient anxieties about unconsecrated bodies that would torment the living as long as they had not fully entered into the realm of the dead:[26] if the dead were not assuaged, were not given peace with a tomb and funerary rites, they could reappear. So it was that the legend evolved that soldiers left buried on the battlefield would explode undetonated shells, as forgotten as they were, wounding and killing passersby in acts of vengeance.[27] Fear of such vengeance can be related to the Breton fears, recorded by ethnologists, of the anger of drowned sailors. Suffering souls were said to haunt the sites of their dramas, eternal purgatories of a sort, seeking satisfaction. Their anger was to be avoided; one had best not linger there.[28]

The guilt of contemporaries toward the dead was later identified, based on the experience of those who escaped genocide, as survivor syndrome; but people felt even guiltier about the missing—the dead without bodies, without rest. On June 18, 1915, the Chamber of Deputies discussed a proposal to deal with this problem by incinerating unidentified bodies. The justification was the need for cleaning and draining the zone of the front. But there was an inconsistency in the distinction between identified veterans, for whom burial remained the rule, and others, who would be reduced to ashes: how was a buried unidentified soldier more likely to threaten public health than a buried soldier whose name was known? In spite of a counterproposal by Deputy Alexandre Lefas, partisans of "the complete removal of bodies" won by 301 votes to 209.[29] The law calling for incineration was never implemented, but one senses in it an unconscious guilt toward the missing and their families, a guilt that preferred reducing the horror to ashes to the countenancing of thousands of anonymous tombs. This had been a "difficult" session, in the opinion of many deputies, and it provoked the ferocious opposition of Catholic traditionalists, for whom the tenet of the resurrection of the body absolutely forbids incineration.[30] Whatever one thinks of the proposal, the missing and the dead were like phantoms who refused to leave the living alone.

The obsession with the resurrection of the dead, the literary evidence shows, did not affect everyone the same way. It fed off two opposing aspirations—of the nationalistic right wing on the one hand, of the socialists and revolutionaries on the other. The theme of the dead guiding the living, of race and blood suffusing the unconscious, of the long chain of generations speaking to contemporaries, had belonged to the right since the end of the nineteenth century. In the right wing's scientific and biological definition of nationalism, neither free will nor independence was possible: sacred law of birthright reigned as a tyrant. "There is no such thing as freedom of thought," wrote Maurice Barrès. "I can live only as my dead lived. They and my soil demand a particular kind of activity."[31] The famous "On your feet, you dead!" of Jacques Péricard, for whom those killed in the agony of the trenches rose up and fired on the enemy, halting their advance, belonged indisputably to this political tradition in the sense that it depicted a nation saved by its dead.[32] The idea of the dead hovering above the battlefields, shedding light on the world of the living with their physical and metaphysical presence, also appears in the work of Drieu la Rochelle. In *La Comédie de Charleroi*, a character guiding a woman searching for the remains of her son declaims, "These souls were hungry and cold and suffering. Something terribly alive, terribly present, rose from the field."[33] And terribly frightening, one might add, since if the dead were suffering, they could give vent to their anger and terrorize the living who had not rendered them the homage that was their due. In 1919 the filmmaker Abel Gance went one step further with his very popular film *J'accuse*, in which the dead appear in the last scene to settle up debts. The title was aimed at the Germans, but the terror evoked by an army of the dead come back to haunt the guilty French who had forgotten them suggests another interpretation. The same rising of the dead, lame and dismembered, occurs in *Le Réveil des morts*, a novel by Roland Dorgelès, in which a selfish widow remarries a veteran, who gradually unmasks his new wife as a woman who cheated on her first soldier-husband when he needed her and then rejoiced at his disappearance. In the last chapter, the new husband accuses his wife:

> It is because you never went there that they never found him. It's you his first glance would have sought when they uncovered his place of burial . . . Are you ever afraid when you think about his letters? . . . He warned you . . . "I love you too much. . . . I will come back! . . . We don't get a burial shroud, so I'll come get mine from your bed. . . ." Now do you remember? . . . From your bed![34]

At that very moment the missing soldier appears at the window, frightening his wife and his replacement to death. In the pages that follow, as in *J'accuse,* the dead reveal themselves, forming a huge army of the forgotten that marches across the country intoning, "What have you done?" The war profiteers, the burial entrepreneurs who made their money on corpses, the women who "lived it up," the politicians always ready to pontificate about homage and aid but who in reality cared nothing at all about the dead and their families—all these selfish characters are struck with panic. France was seized with fear at the prospect of punishment, of these soldiers come back for justice, the justice that was owed them and never rendered.

In contrast to this vision of guilt, in which the dead condemned a society that had forgotten those who had sacrificed themselves for it, the socialists envisioned the dead who reappeared claiming vengeance as turning their fury on the military, the capitalists, and other war profiteers. Instead of a nation betrayed by base behavior, they saw the union of all the proletarians from all the battlefields making common cause against militaristic and nationalistic warmongers. On both sides, in other words, there was a settling of debts, and the dead were recruited for the cause. Pacifism ran the political spectrum in the period between the two world wars, and the theme of the dead as guardians of the peace also appeared in the nonsocialist press. Witness Jean Suberville's poem drawn from the *Journal des mutilés,* in which the dead rise up for a new vigil, reminding humanity of the horror of war and the happiness of peace.[35] That was also the theme of a poem by A. Salis, which took the socialist view of the waking of the dead. Those responsible for the catastrophe are named, and the international community of the dead is summoned to fight for a humanity threatened by "assassins":

> *When all that lives is praying,*
> *When all that moves is sleeping,*
> *Opening wide their giant coffins*
> *They awaken—the dead!*
> *Bloody, piled and jumbled together,*
> *There they are, in the twilight,*
> *Eyes haggard, limbs twisted,*
> *Horrible sleepwalkers,*
> *Specters of terror,*
> *Unspeakable remains*

THE LIVING UNKNOWN SOLDIER

Covered with gaping wounds,
They were fellow creatures.

Country, honor and mercenaries,
Profiteers, large or small,
Admire those years of poverty and horror—
This is your picture of honor.

Oh! Fierce patriots,
Impetuous killers,
You that nothing moves,
Neither the widow nor the orphan,
And for whom the war
Is the noblest of games,
Approach their shrouds,
Listen to them a bit.

There is no longer a border
Separating them as before,
And under the cold stone,
They are brothers now,
From France or from Germany,
From Italy, from Great Britain,
Serbs, Belgians, Hungarians,
Russians, Austrians, Bavarians,
All have finally understood,
That they were your victims,
And that the words honor, country,
Only hide your crimes.

And this sinister spectacle
In the fading light of the day,
Oh! the emperors, presidents, ministers,
They throw in your face
The title that destiny
Forever reserves for you: assassin!
And in a powerful voice,
That is heard everywhere,
To the ignorant multitudes,
They cry: Educate yourselves.
To keep the world from once again,
Tomorrow, turning into
A filthy charnel house,
A meal for human vultures,
The wretched of the earth
Must rise up, uttering this cry:
"We have only one enemy: poverty,
Only one country: the universe!" [36]

Gigi Damiano's anarchist lampoon, *L'Histoire du Soldat inconnu* (*The Story of the Unknown Soldier*), went even further. It did not stop with having the dead talking, or even commanding; it had them marching, like the dead in *J'accuse* and *Le Réveil des morts*—in this case, toward social revolution. Damiano concocted a life for the Unknown Soldier. A proletarian forced to go to war, who calls for solidarity and is killed in a volley of friendly fire, he prophesies the grand revolt of the victims of capitalism, dead and alive together, guided in their just cause by a sacred icon, the nation:

But the day will come, O unknown soldiers from every battle,
O anonymous heroes who gave others their fortune,
A day will come when I will shatter the gravestone,
When I will take the lead at the head of all those who come to tell me
—in hushed voices,
So that no one will accuse them of treason—
That they've been tricked . . . duped . . . robbed.
At the head of peasant soldiers who had no land,
Of worker soldiers who had no factory,
Of citizen soldiers who had no city—
All the cripples who have no tomorrow.
And I will rally you, you too,
Unknown soldiers, soldiers without names in life as in death,
Skeletons pulled from the wartime trenches of every day.
And I will call out to all the unknowns who are still alive.
And all together, we will march . . . we will leave . . .
Once again . . .
Woe to the living when the dead awaken.[37]

As late as 1998, in a children's book called *Zap the War,* the artist Pef shows an army of the lame streaming out of a monument to the war dead, eighty years on, to find out whether indeed they died for nought. They discover, to their bitterness, that wars are still being waged, and that the lessons of yesterday have never been understood.[38] There is no question but that the French of the twenties and thirties, whether on the right or on the left, lived with the dead, haunted by them and yet anguished at the thought of forgetting them while they themselves continued to live.

The theme of the amnesic soldier was closely linked to that of the dead soldier. The former was like one of the living dead, utterly removed from the world and indifferent to the passions that move it. Critic Carine Trévisan called amnesia a "death by loss of identity."[39] Distant and detached, shut off from all clues to his identity, the amnesiac was simultaneously outside the war and a product of it. And so the theme of the amnesiac, who was like an accusation to those who had not lost their memory or who had gone mad from remembering too much, fascinated writers. From William Faulkner's first novel, *Soldier's Pay*,[40] to Jean Giraudoux's *Siegfried et le Limousin* and the theater of Pirandello, amnesia lay at the heart of the literature written between the two wars.[41]

Whether he was an unconscious spectator at his own drama, a tortured wreck around whom the living gathered (like Faulkner's soldier, Donald Mahon), or the fully conscious protagonist of his story (like Giraudoux's counselor, Siegfried), the amnesic soldier shouldered his contemporaries' guilt, his very existence condemning war and its absurdity. Considered mad "by those who lacked imagination,"[42] amnesiacs were often presented as the only truly free individuals that the horror of European history had produced. Abel Moreau's novel *Le Fou* (*The Madman*) provides one of the clearest instances. It tells the story of an amnesiac who recovers his memory—and then uses it to keep his fellow sufferers from recovering theirs, since reality is too hard to bear.[43] In Giraudoux and Anouilh one finds the same praise for oblivion, for the purity of amnesia as a second birth. The man without a past is a man without hate. "I am a German child, six years old," says Giraudoux's Siegfried,[44] who is found naked on the battlefield and reeducated as a German. Gaston, Anouilh's "traveler without luggage," lashes out at the society that is forcing him to uncover his past and his family when what he really wants is to retain his virginal present, without hatred and without prejudice:

> No doubt it frightened people that a man can live without a past. Even before the war, people didn't like foundlings. . . . But after all, there's time to shape them a little. But a man, an adult man with no country, no birthplace, no traditions, no name . . . Damn! What a scandal! . . .
>
> I was so peaceful in the asylum. . . . I was used to myself, I knew myself well. And now they want me to leave myself, to find another self and put him on like an old jacket. Would I recognize myself tomorrow, I who drink nothing but water, in the son of a lamplighter who needs no less than a gallon of red wine a day? Or I, a man with no patience at all, in the son of a notions merchant who collects and sorts twelve hundred kinds of buttons by category?[45]

In contrast to the authors who praised oblivion—or peace through oblivion, to use Harald Weinrich's expression[46]— Jean Bommart, who was fascinated with spiritualism and communication with the dead, chose to go upstream on the Lethe, that river in hell that dispenses oblivion to the deceased. In *Le Revenant* (*The Ghost*), he traces the story of a peaceable and methodical bank clerk who leads a dreary life until, following an automobile accident, he finds himself projected from 1931 back to 1917. Disoriented by the experience, he is unable, upon his return, to pick up his former life, which he sees now as gray and boring. Lazy, violent, and drawn to Bolshevism, he no longer resembles the man he was. His wife is frightened: he is a a stranger to her, and when night comes she feels as though she is cheating on her husband with a new lover. Ultimately the man can find no peace except with one old comrade who has not changed and to whom he can talk about the inexplicable experiences of the war and the repressed memories that suddenly surface.[47] It is not pleasant to come back, though, swimming upstream; Bommart's soldier pays for his return to the bohemian days of his youth with ill health and lost social position. More than seventy years earlier, in *L'Homme à l'oreille cassée* (*The Man with the Broken Ear*), a novel largely drawn from *Colonel Chabert*, Edmond About had shown how difficult it was to live in the future with the framework of the past. "A man must live in his era. Later, it's too late," asserts the main character, a colonel of the Empire who is dissected by a Prussian scientist in 1812 and brought back to life fifty years later.[48] His return cannot be, and the novel ends, tragically, with his suicide: he no longer has a place in a new world that has forged ahead without him.

Jean Giraudoux was among the most prestigious authors to use the myth of the man who comes back. His novel *Siegfried et le Limousin,* published by Grasset in 1922 and adapted for the stage in 1927, treats amnesia as a political problem. Steeped in German culture and no doubt deeply torn, not to mention wounded and disabled, during the war, Giraudoux was haunted by questions of remembering and forgetting. The attacks of amnesia that his brother suffered on his return from the war must have impressed him, and he dedicated his *Lectures pour une ombre* (*Readings for a Shadow*), a collection of war stories that he published in 1917, to "André du Fresnois, missing." With *Siegfried,* Giraudoux demonstrated the absurdity of war and brought the two warring nations together in the person of the writer Jacques Forestier, declared missing after being wounded in the head and found, naked and totally amnesic, on the battlefield. He learns German from the nurse who rescues him; he is baptized Siegfried; later on he works on the creation of the new Germany's constitution. Both French and German, he is the man with two pasts, the two enemy cultures united in a wedding of blood. Even when informed by his relatives of his true identity, he refuses to deny this double heritage, which makes him a link between the two nations. In the 1927 stage adaptation he says,

> Siegfried and Forestier will live side by side. I will try to bear honorably the two names and the two destinies that chance has given me. . . . I refuse to dig trenches inside myself. I will return to France not as the last prisoner released from a German prison but as the first beneficiary of a new science, or a new heart. . . .[49]

But hatred for Germany was still very much alive in the twenties, and Siegfried's enterprise of reconciliation was quite bold: the amnesiac was not always the link between the two peoples that Giraudoux had envisioned. Witness Marcel Priollet's novel *Veuves blanches* (*White Widows*), in which Jeannine, a young woman who has never accepted the death of her fiancé, René, sets out on July 20, 1918, on a veritable detective hunt to trace him. After swearing fidelity to him in the section allotted to the missing in the cemetery—"He will find me the way he left me. His place is here, in my heart, always . . ."[50]—she writes to René's officers and to the members of his company. She travels to the site where he disappeared, learning that through a mistake in identification he was taken captive, wounded and amnesic, in Neustadt. From the testimony of former prisoners in the camp, she discovers that he soon escaped and passed out while crossing the Rhine; after that he was taken in by a Swiss-German family who attempted a Machiavellian re-creation of his identity into that of a German deserter—considering the transformation of a Frenchman into a German a kind of revenge—and rebaptizing him Rheinfisch. In a fantastic episode, Jeannine abruptly removes René from the machinations of the enemy by kidnapping him. The restaging of their last tender meeting, in the same spot, with the same words and the same clothes, restores to the amnesiac both his memory and his loyal Jeannine. A kind of anti-*Siegfried*, this cumbersome novel cultivated a refusal to forget, or to resign oneself to mourning, and encouraged the vain hope of seeing the missing return.[51]

Anthelme Mangin embodied just such a possibility. With him, the soldier who returned left the realms of fiction. "Why couldn't a moving novel by Marcel Priollet become reality?" asked *La Voix des combattants* in 1928.[52] The notion was all the more credible because Anthelme Mangin was not the only unidentified amnesiac. In Italy there was another nameless soldier, interned in a psychiatric hospital, caught between two families who claimed him as their own, and he, too, became a source of inspiration for writers.

The Collegno amnesiac, who was as famous in Italy as Mangin was unsung in France, became the object of a 1981 study by Leonardo Sciascia titled *The Theater of Memory*.[53] Unable to furnish his identity after he was arrested in Turin for petty larceny in 1926, he was interned in the asylum at Collegno and his portrait published in the Sunday supplement of the *Corriere della sera*.[54] Among the many families who thought they recognized him, two took their claim to an all but interminable trial, which from 1928 to 1931 produced 142 witnesses and the testimony of 14 experts. One Signora Canella recognized her husband, a distinguished professor who had gone missing on the eastern front, and one Signora Bruneri *her* husband, a lowlife crook. The putative amnesiac, who chose the Canellas—acquiring thereby a substantial fortune and a loving wife, whom he soon enough impregnated—was finally identified through fingerprints: he was indeed the petty thief Bruneri. But the Canella family persisted, against all logic, and continued, from exile in Brazil, to avow their certainty. This case of expropriation of identity impassioned Italy for several years[55] and stimulated the imagination of Luigi Pirandello. Fascinated by the theme of memory and oblivion, which he first put onstage in *The Late Mattia Pascal* (1904), in which the hero talks even though he is dead, he returned to the genre with *Right You Are (If You Think You Are),* which was directly inspired by the Bruneri-Canella case. Published in 1930 and mounted for the first time in France in 1932, Pirandello's play relates the story of an amnesic woman gone missing after the invasion of the Udine region by the Austrians in 1917, and presents identity as an amalgam of what one thinks one is and what others think. The amnesiac, recognized by the Pieri family ten years after the disappearance, is confronted in the final scene by a repulsive madwoman who may very well be the actual relative in question. Convinced that indeed she is, the amnesiac introduces the madwoman to them herself, shaking the convictions of those who had identified her and who are repelled to see in this poor wreck the beautiful Lucia of before:

> More than one unhappy person, after several years, has come back in this state [*she shows the madwoman*] . . . her face now almost inhuman . . . unrecognizable without her memory . . . and sisters, wives, mothers . . . mothers . . . fight over him! "He's mine!"—"No, he's mine!" . . . and that isn't because he looks like their missing person. No! The son of one can't possibly be like someone else's! . . . But because they *believed* it was him! They wanted to believe it! . . . And when one wants to believe, no proof to the contrary will hold up! . . . It's not him? . . . But for this mother, yes, it's him! What difference does it make if it's not him, if this mother keeps him and, with all her love, makes him hers? . . . In spite of all the evidence, she believes it. . . . Me, didn't you believe in me without proof?[56]

Since the madwoman turns out to be the true Lucia Pieri, Pirandello asks the question that, over and above the desire to believe in spite of everything and contrary to all evidence, explains all the mistakes and the deceptions: How does one recognize a loved one missing for so many years—by the fact that he hasn't changed or, rather, by the fact that he *has*?

This is the "foolish ingeniousness" of the title character in "The Improbable Impostor Tom Castro," a short story by Jorge Luis Borges—who, writing at the beginning of the thirties, also knew about the Bruneri-Canella affair. Eleven years after the steamship *Mermaid* has gone down in the middle of the Atlantic and with her the officer Charles Tichborne, his mother, a very rich Englishwoman, continues to believe that he has survived, publishing tearful pleas in the newspapers. The idea of Tom Castro, "a dumpy lout" with a reddish complexion, is to pass himself off as Lady Tichborne's lost son, even though the son was svelte, well proportioned, and olive skinned: "The very enormity of the pretense would be convincing proof that it wasn't a trick."[57] In the event, he is welcomed with open arms by the inconsolable Englishwoman, and no one dares contradict her, because "everyone knows that a mother doesn't make such mistakes."

Where Pirandello and Borges borrowed from the Collegno amnesiac, Anouilh took his inspiration from Anthelme Mangin, baptizing his hero without a past "the living unknown soldier." The series of ten articles by Paul Bringuier that appeared in *L'Intransigeant* in May 1935 were probably the source for *The Traveler without Luggage,* first performed on

February 16, 1937, at the Théâtre des Mathurins. Anouilh pursued the notion he had explored in *There Was a Prisoner* (1935), in which a swindler emerging from fifteen years in prison discovers, to his disgust, that his relatives are all comfortably housed, sated, hypocritical, and anxious for respectability, and chooses flight with another freed prisoner over remaining with them. *The Traveler without Luggage* was lavishly praised by critics, and the play's connection with Anthelme Mangin did not escape the attention of Robert de Beauplan, the critic for *La Petite Illustration:* "The idea doesn't seem unbelievable at all. The daily newspapers have written enough about the Rodez amnesiac for us to be convinced of the possibility of such a case."[58] Gaston, the main character, is an amnesiac discovered in a triage station in the spring of 1918 after climbing off a convoy of repatriates from Germany. Since then he has been in a psychiatric hospital, where everyone is trying, by every means possible, to discover his identity. But he is indifferent, even fearful, because he is no longer the same man. He is claimed by several dozen families and contemplates with detachment the comings and goings of those who suffer from too much remembering; his sole desire is to be left in peace with this new self of his. Confronted by the Renaud family, which turns out to be his real family, he discovers that before being reborn as a Siegfried-like amnesiac he was a loathsome fellow who tortured animals, chased after maids, seduced his sister-in-law, and had plenty of gambling debts but no friends. His mother, furious at his loutishness, may not even have kissed him good-bye when he left for the war; in short, an awful family and, as for him, a creep. But the "traveler without luggage" rejects this heritage, choosing instead to lie about recognizing a little boy with no family with whom to build his future, because his own past is far too ugly. Starting from the idea that forgetting is the opportunity for a new beginning, Anouilh presents Gaston as the only truly free man, the only man capable of denying his past. To his mistress, who disagrees—"You can't deny yourself"—the amnesiac replies, "I'm probably the only man, it's true, that destiny has given the chance to live everybody's dream. . . . I'm a man, but if I want I can be as new as a baby! It's a privilege it would be criminal not to use. It's *you* I deny."[59]

Anthelme Mangin's case was entirely different. The Rodez amnesiac was not a free man at all, and his negativism was merely an aspect of his dementia. He was incapable of expressing irony, of choosing, or even of reasoning, and his life as a patient from 1918 until his death in 1942 was a tragedy, while *The Traveler without Luggage* and *Right You Are* vacillated between comedy and tragedy without ever really becoming one or the other.[60]

What had worked well in the theater, with a first-rate script, was a flop on film. The 1944 adaptation of *The Traveler without Luggage,* under the direction of Anouilh himself, had a poor critical reception, despite the talent that Pierre Fresnay displayed in the title role. The mixture of drama and vaudeville put off the public. By that time, the theme of returning soldiers, whether dead, or missing, or as amnesiacs reborn on the battlefield—as frightening specters come back

from the void or as new men rising from the hell of combat—
no longer wielded the power it had between the two wars,
when the guilt of the living toward the war dead was at its
height. Anthelme Mangin, who had died in obscurity two
years previously, the man who even in literature had been the
symbol of France in mourning, part cult of memory, part
elegy for oblivion, was almost completely forgotten.

Chapter Four

The Pilgrimage to Rodez

From all corners of France—from Brittany to Corsica, from Franche-Comté to Algeria and farther abroad—a flood of suffering relatives converged on the Rodez asylum. The Rodez departmental archives have preserved files on and letters from 292 families who requested either information about Anthelme Mangin or permission to meet him. And it is clear that there were many more: leaving aside the hysterical estimates in the press of 5,000 letters received by the asylum in the week following the publication of Mangin's photograph and the fanciful notion of the postman's having to deliver the mail in a wheelbarrow,[1] it is still certain that a considerable portion of the correspondence has disappeared. Witness this passage from a letter of Fenayrou to the prefect on March 26, 1926, explaining the delays in answering families' letters: "This is the 366th letter I have written since the end of February regarding the patient Mangin, the greatest number of which required examination of the patient, of detailed comparative samples of writing, and of photographs. I have, in addition, played host to forty families who have come to the asylum to see the patient." As each of these meetings lasted several hours, one can imagine how over-worked the director was. But his duties relating to the identification of Mangin were not always so intense; they oscillated between relative calm and the overwhelming activity that followed every new series of articles in the large dailies. After each of these journalistic investigations, whether they included a picture of the patient or not, dozens of bereaved relatives claimed to recognize him or requested a better photograph before deciding.

Most of the letter writers were women. Out of a hundred letters the asylum received in April 1922, sixty-nine came from women. Of the total known requests, one in seven concerned a missing brother, one in five a husband, and one in two a son who had never returned from the war.[2] Almost all the initial letters began with a reference to the daily that had made the writer aware of the case, and many ordinary people, for whom writing a letter was a chore, got help from an intermediary—most often the mayor of their town, but sometimes their deputy, an official they had elected and in whom they had confidence, such as the Réunion deputy Boussenot, who went to Rodez himself at the request of a constituent who could not make the trip.[3] Prefects were also asked and, more rarely, the local secretaries of veterans' organizations, as well as priests. All of France was represented. The requests came from every corner of the country—from Brittany, Corrèze, Poitou, Paris,

Corsica, as well as Algeria and New Caledonia—and from every social class. "Peasant women in regional headdress and in large heavy shoes, working women with broken fingernails and hair cropped short, and well-off ladies with fine stockings,"[4] as one journal reported, could all be found at the asylum's front gate.

When foreign magazines published articles about Mangin, the same thing happened. On March 23, 1922, a Swiss citizen named Maurice Dubois wrote to Rodez about a son who had volunteered for the French army and disappeared in May 1915. In October 1922, a Mrs. Harrison of Penarth, England, thought she recognized her husband in "the man with no name." Her file was quickly rejected, since her husband had gone missing in May 1918 and Mangin had been discovered and interned since February 1918. Later, on May 17, 1928, the day after an article about Mangin appeared in the *Daily Mirror*, the French consulate in Southampton received a request and transmitted it to the Aveyron prefect. But it led nowhere; nor did one from a woman in Guernsey in July. A claim came in from Latvia, but Mangin had no moles or growths in the places it mentioned.[5] The German soldier Christian Seidenberg, subject of a request transmitted by the German embassy to the Ministry of Foreign Affairs, and from there to Pensions, also turned out to be a false lead; the request, from Koblenz, ignored the facts that the Rodez patient spoke only French (with minimal notions of English) and that his height was different. The case of René Rondot, a French Canadian from Prince Albert who volunteered on December 30, 1914—to the despair of his parents, who never heard from him again—was less clear-cut. Dr. Locard, an expert in graphology and the director of the police laboratory in Lyon, formally identified his handwriting as that of Mangin on February 15, 1926. But his evidence hardly mattered, since Rondot was five feet eight, nearly four inches taller than Mangin. So Fenayrou rejected the claim. In February and March 1929, the claims of a Mrs. Savage and a Mrs. Hughston of Ottawa and Long Branch, Ontario, respectively, ended the same way.

In their letters, the families recounted their continuing efforts to find their relatives. "I have written everywhere," confided the widow Rondin, on February 27, 1936. "My husband has been missing since October 26, 1914; I have tried everything to find him," began a letter from Mme. Lecaille-Wimet of Boulogne-sur-Mer.[6] The tales of all these efforts, which did nothing to identify Mangin and so were useless to the director of the asylum, underlined how constant the affection for the missing remained, as if having kept the soldier in their heart was in itself part of what might make the case for the kind of miracle that would bring him back. Jeanne Mangin, of Saint-Brieuc, who spoke of the Rodez amnesiac as her husband, insisted on her love as if it were an argument: "I'd like to know about the mental state of my husband, Anthelme Mangin. Is there any possibility that he could come home . . . where he could see his wife and his children, who have always loved him?"[7] The mourning that had scarcely begun stopped abruptly when people heard about Mangin. The slowly repressed pain surged back forcefully, for all hope was not lost. There was still one last place to search. It was a duty:

Since 1914 I have been looking for my son, who was inducted in 1913. . . . I have done the most meticulous research throughout the French sectors and in German camps. A fruitless search, but when I read this article, my duty as a mother came back anew: to see whether I might find the child I am looking for in this unfortunate man.[8]

Many hopefuls still seeking their missing relatives had never started the process of mourning. Their suffering had continued unabated since the disappearance—at least, when they had not descended straight into madness, as in the case of the grandmother of Antoine Gaudin, from Marseille, whose family became interested in Anthelme Mangin at the beginning of the thirties.[9] A Mme. Tugnaire of Paris wrote, "Since 1914, it's been a perpetual ordeal. Have pity on me. . . . I see in *Le Matin* that one of these poor martyrs is in Rodez. Could it be my little one gone missing when he was leading his men in an assault?"[10] The widow Venzac, from Maisons-Alfort, near Paris, lost her two sons in the war and so hoped to find "her Marcel" in Mangin that she came to fear the trip to Rodez; what if "it turned out to be too big a disappointment"?[11] But hope revived was an ordeal in itself. Just as in the days following the disappearance of her sons, now she waited for the postman bearing Fenayrou's answer with impatience: "Every day I tell myself it will come tomorrow, and I hear nothing."[12] In the end, suffering won over hope: "I ask you only . . . to tell me the truth, no matter how painful, to get me out of this nightmare."[13] Like her, Mme. Loucke Allemersch, of Roubaix, realized a few days after writing enthusiastically on April 7 and 13, 1922, how little hope there was of finding her husband, and she decided to think it over before undertaking a trip to Rodez that ran the risk of doing her more harm than good.[14]

Mme. Allemersch was, however, a reasonable woman, capable of reflecting on her situation—which was not always the case with those who authoritatively affirmed that Mangin was their relative. Granted, the most prudent among them recognized the effects of passing time and, consequently, hesitated: "There is a resemblance, but he is much older. It's true that ten years have passed, and this poor man must have suffered so much."[15] But others swept away their doubts. "We were taken, my mother and I," wrote a young woman from Belfort in 1935, "by the resemblance, which, despite many years having gone by, allows us to hope for the good fortune of finding the one we continue to believe despite everything is still alive."[16] "For me, there is no doubt—he is my son!" a Mme. Pierson echoed three months later.[17] A woman named Ceccaldi, from Osani, in Corsica, offered an argument that she considered irrefutable: "A mother can't be mistaken, and I certainly recognized him."[18] Strengthened by her conviction that the legitimacy of her claim was incontestable, she was sure that Louise Vayssettes would soon give up her claim to Mangin's guardianship: "This family that thinks they recognize him as their son will soon acknowledge their error."[19] Where others might be mistaken, her own resolve was unquestionable. Similarly, Victor Rieux felt sorry for the "unfortunate families who think they have recognized one of their own" when Mangin was none other than his brother

Eugène, as he formally declared in February 1935.[20] When it was helpful, irrational measures could be called on to bolster conviction. Louise Vayssettes, for example, sought counsel from a fortune-teller to be sure she had really found her brother, Albert Mazenc.[21] For her part, Mme. Pierson, who always refused to accept the death of the son killed by shrapnel on December 20, 1916, knew that Mangin showed the trace of a former fracture to his right leg, and she brought in a medium to support her for lack of any other identifying proof:

> Certainly great physicians have recognized that in spite of separation, a certain fluid or mystical communication connects a real mother and her child. As for me, with no news of my child, in a dream I saw him taken prisoner; then I saw him make a long trip on foot. He was hungry! And as he passed by he held out his hand, and gentle hearts gave him bread, which he wolfed down. Afterward, much later, I dreamed he was in a battlefield—not one in France—and all of a sudden he was wounded in the leg. I saw him hopping along on a wooden leg.[22]

But these were merely dreams taken for truth. The ordeal did not end there. Following the model of Pirandello's *Right You Are,* families recognized Mangin because they were ready to recognize practically anybody. Contemplating the photo of the amnesiac, all of them were struck by the resemblance to their relative—a resemblance that existed only in the obstinate wills of those in need. Fenayrou, who had pushed to see the case resolved by involving the press, found himself caught in his own trap. In January 1923, having just lived through a highly stressful year, his tone was despairing: "I fear that the mystery of my poor patient's identity is nowhere close to being solved."[23] From then on, until his retirement, in 1935, he was condemned to apply his expertise to one after another request to evaluate the resemblance, to compare physical characteristics and handwriting, to search Mangin's body for distinguishing marks.

The full-face and profile photographs posted on the doors of city halls were accompanied by a notice that turned out to be largely ineffective. Anthelme Mangin was then about thirty years old; he was five feet four and a half; his hair, his beard, and his eyes were brown; his forehead displayed the beginnings of baldness; his ears did not protrude; his skin was pale; his face was round. Three characteristics in particular were noted. His right tibia was deformed, as a result of a fracture in the lower third. He had a half-circle scar on his left wrist. And he had freckles on his face. The notice added that "he appears to have received a secondary education";[24] it had become apparent, during the course of dictation tests in different languages, that he knew some English.

But most of the relatives who wrote in took little account of this information, which was, in any case, too general to identify anyone with. "The notice, the way it was usually written, did not lend itself to individuation," as Suzanne Vigneron remarked in her 1937 law thesis on the legal protection of identity. "Average nose, average mouth, round chin, and oval face are the terms used most often. They could apply to anyone."[25] Seizing on the case of Anthelme Mangin, she proposed preventing further dramas like that of the Rodez amnesiac by introducing an identity card with fingerprints that would amount to the transfer of "bertillonization" from the penal realm to the civil. The word refers to the work of Alphonse Bertillon, who, beginning in 1882, created a scientific approach to police work[26] by establishing a system of identification based on anthropometry, the study of comparative human measurements. Offenders were henceforth to be categorized by having their bones measured and their fingerprints conserved. But the factor that had brought the Bruneri-Canella affair in Italy to a close, the exposure of the impostor Bruneri by his fingerprints, bore no fruit in the case of Mangin, an upstanding man with no police record.

The press reported on the inquiry's progress with unstinting sensationalism, upsetting Fenayrou's work by continuing to publish Mangin's photograph as late as 1937, when it was no longer current and would lead to bitter disappointments. Rapid dispatches passed along by other papers, based sometimes on facts and sometimes on hopeful relatives' version of the facts, not to mention the inventions of the journalists themselves, all combined to mislead those with an interest in the story rather than to inform them. On March 9, 1922, Fenayrou complained to the prefect about the press's exaggerated reports of Mangin's education; his language tests had been peppered with mistakes. With the goal of protecting his patient, and conscientiously hewing to his work as an expert, the asylum director refused to brief the press himself. To the queries of a journalist from *Le Progrès de Lyon,* who in

February 1926 asked him for information about the new case of the Canadian soldier Rondot, Fenayrou declined to comment, invoking doctor-patient privilege. Taking his task to heart, he personally endeavored to reply to letters from families, quickly eliminating requests that were off base for obvious reasons (the age of the missing person, his height, the color of his hair or his eyes, the date of his disappearance); he sent a better picture to others before they had decided whether to travel to Rodez. Compassionate and touched by their grief, the director did not hesitate to invite relatives with doubts to come meet Mangin in order to decide for sure, even when he had no illusions himself about the validity of their requests.

Unfortunately, all too often he got little thanks for his efforts. For each case he agreed to look into, he requested a photograph, a handwriting sample, and a description of the missing man in question. For better precision, or in cases when the relatives failed to send the requested documents, he wrote to the military office that had recruited the missing person in order to secure the kind of descriptive material the army required, which was more reliable than the memories of the relatives writing him. For Fenayrou in his capacity as expert, pictures, letters, and postcards were the tools of his work; but for the families who sent them, they were precious souvenirs, all the more so because they were often the last letters they had received. Thus the Canadians François and Catherine Rondot sent Fenayrou their son's final letter, in which he explained why he had volunteered for the war: "Now I am twenty-one years old and I think I have given you enough trouble, but I couldn't leave it at that. . . . Oh, dear Mama, dry your tears. I'll come back. If I hadn't left, I would have gotten sick. I ask your forgiveness for the trouble I've given you; pray for me a little, it will help me."[27] When her request was turned down, Mme. Betton from Pailhares, in Ardèche, got her mayor to help her retrieve "the only souvenir this family has of our lost son."[28] The widow Venzac, who enclosed postcards with her letter, found the right words: "I will be grateful if you return all these pitiful objects which are so precious to me."[29]

When the descriptions matched and the resemblance to Mangin was obvious, Fenayrou examined the handwriting and, although he was not a specialist, made every effort to discern its characteristics. All the cases that actually made it to trial would require an examination by an independent expert, such as Professor Raymond Sorel, a professor of medical law at the University of Toulouse, brought in by the Ministry of Pensions in 1923 and 1926 to decide on the assertions of first nine, and then eleven families, all of whose claims he rejected. But Sorel was not really a specialist in the field. Starting in 1926, graphologists were brought in to provide expert advice on the most problematic cases, notably those of Lemay and Monjoin. Still, what with diverging opinions and the limitations of the method, identification could not be established based solely on their conclusions. Graphology, which had pretensions toward positioning itself as a new science, had been a craze toward the end of the nineteenth century, converting psychologists, physiologists, and hypnotists eager to identify the true personality of their patients via their handwriting.[30] This new means of ferreting out symptoms, often under hypnosis, also found its way into the judicial domain, even if judges were often cautious about its claims. The experts, it was well known, had been mistaken in the Dreyfus affair, which discredited both them and graphology.

Dr. Edmond Locard, the director of the Lyon police laboratory, who may be considered the true inventor of an ostensibly scientific graphology, gave the field new life. Before him, resemblances and differences between writing samples were simply accumulated, and a decision made. But after the publication of his definitive *Criminal Investigation and Scientific Methods*,[31] experts measured the spaces between letters, the gaps, and the height and variation of lowercase letters, establishing an index grid of, for example, the curving arches of the letters *n*, *m*, and *u*. The curves were superimposed on the writing samples, and matchups could then be easily determined.[32] Unfortunately, notwithstanding its great scientific appeal, the Locard method failed miserably in the case of the Rodez amnesiac. Asked to evaluate Rondot's handwriting in 1925, Edmond Locard traveled to Aveyron and dictated two letters to Mangin[33]—not without difficulty, since the patient wrote in a trembling and irregular hand. Despite what Locard called "inhibitions," he noted, in his fourteen remarks, similar mistakes of syntax and spelling, identical spacing between the lines, the same stroke at the beginning of letters, a final rising stroke in both men's handwriting, and a common accentuation of the letter *s*. On February 15, 1926, he delivered his verdict: "One can conclude that the author of the letters signed by René Rondot is indeed the author of the dictations made in the Rodez asylum"—much to Fenayrou's consternation, since the director had not found on Mangin's forehead the scar that Rondot's relatives remembered, nor the same teeth, and on top of that the missing man had been much taller than Mangin. Locard loved relating his exploits in his many books, but he never had much to say about this total misidentification.[34] Afterward, when Fenayrou needed a handwriting expert, he deliberately overlooked Locard in favor of M. Samaran, who was attached to the court in the department of Seine.

For the present, though, Fenayrou was no further along, and the best way for him and for the families to make a determination remained face-to-face meetings with Mangin. Contrary to what Paul Bringuier reported in *L'Intransigeant*, they were not held in groups;[35] bringing together fifty people, all stretching their arms out toward the amnesiac and calling him different names in complete chaos, would have accomplished nothing. The visits were strictly individual, with families scheduling them after being authorized by the Ministry of Pensions to meet the unknown man. Until 1928, the ministry granted these authorizations fairly easily, on receipt of a simple request. When a family knocked at the asylum door without the necessary approval, Fenayrou sidestepped the procedure and sent them on to the prefecture.

The meetings always followed the same procedure. The asylum director received the applicant or applicants in his office. He listened as they expressed their hopes and doubts, then asked them to list all the particular characteristics they could remember, the essential elements for making an identification. Fenayrou had encountered the most far-fetched assurances by convinced relatives, who in their letters would hasten to find reasons that such and such a trait of Mangin's described in the press failed to correspond to their own missing person. Mangin knew a bit of English; the Pierson son didn't speak a word of it. His mother argued nevertheless: "He could have had a comrade who spoke English, or else found himself in an English camp, or else been a prisoner in Germany with Englishmen."[36] Jean Dikous, an Algerian Kabyle who had settled in Compiègne, had another explanation for Mangin's silence and incoherent sentences: if he said "I don't know" to the questions of police interrogators and doctors, it was simply because the unidentified man in whom he hoped to find his cousin didn't speak French well. Mangin's name would have been his army commander's, and in any case, "the man hospitalized in Rodez looks more or less Algerian."[37] Even more absurd were the hypotheses of Victor Rieux, who said that his missing brother knew the city of Rodez very well, having done his military service there;[38] and of a Mme. Gastaud-Ivaldi, who insisted that her brother was without his identification papers when he was found because he had lost his wallet a few days before going missing.[39]

On another front, Fenayrou encouraged efforts to discover the profession Mangin had practiced before he was drafted. According to Jean Aicardi, a reporter who wrote an investigative series for *Le Petit Marseillais,* published from May 21 to May 25 and September 8 through September 15, 1931, all kinds of tools and instruments were given to Mangin in the attempt to determine his profession—a wasted effort, as "Anthelme Mangin never made the slightest movement, the slightest gesture."[40] To uncover (at the request of several families) any agricultural talent Mangin might have, Fenayrou sent him out with a sickle to do some reaping on the asylum grounds—another failure. The amnesiac was incapable of any activity.[41] For once a journalistic report was something more than pure invention, as Jean Aicardi went to Rodez personally and met some of the drama's protagonists—unlike Paul Bringuier, who in 1935 seized upon the articles from *Le Petit Marseillais,* adding to the reported interrogations with his own narrative abilities. (It was not likely, as *L'Intransigeant* reported, that Fenayrou, already so alienated from the press, would have authorized anyone to try to hypnotize Mangin into pronouncing his real name.)[42]

After scrupulously noting the particular characteristics indicated by the families, the asylum director would send for the amnesiac and verify, in front of them, the presence or absence of the marks. But it was rare for off-base claimants, even when discouraged by the procedure, to abandon their hopes and end the meeting there, though this did happen on a couple of occasions.[43] The director was also diligent about writing down everyone's reactions, including the patient's. He stayed off to one side during the meeting but remained present from beginning to end. The patient's appearance was always a shock. Some visitors were stupefied, or else, showing their doubt, they scrutinized him attentively. But those who made up their minds immediately were demonstrative—they extended their arms toward Mangin, they caressed him, they gave him presents, they overwhelmed him with tender words, with tears, or with long monologues containing endless lists of familiar places, friends and relatives, and memories of happy times, of childhood, or of peacetime. They spoke to him in every possible dialect. They showed him photographs or objects charged with meaning.

Nothing brought the amnesiac out of his torpor. Yet he was not completely immobile. He might take an interest in the pictures on postcards or touch the objects or the buttons on the coats of his supposed relatives. But he was largely indifferent; once, sitting on a bench, he went to sleep during a meeting. The asylum director tried giving him letters addressed to him by people who claimed him, "in hopes of awakening his memory"[44] and of getting "a glimmer of intelligence"[45] from him—no reaction. Reading material didn't interest him, either, and he took no pleasure in the packages sent to him. He was indifferent to sweets. He seemed to want nothing. Repeated meetings disturbed him, as did prolonged dictation tests. Almost every time he had to remove his clothing so that visitors could see the presence or absence of the identifying marks they had mentioned, he showed some irritation; but at Fenayrou's calm insistence, he would comply wordlessly. After examining him as if he were some strange animal, one grief-stricken mother insisted that he open his mouth to see whether he wasn't missing an incisor, like her son Paul. Despite Mangin's reluctance and Fenayrou's protests that Mangin had all his incisors, they had to satisfy her in order to erase her illusions.[46] (Information supplied by Marthe Mazat about a possible scar on her son's penis, however, was not verified.)[47] Mostly silent, the amnesiac might offer incoherent replies, affirmative or negative—which would throw off even the most enthusiastic seekers, though they would pretend afterward that they had been recognized—or he would pronounce a few incomprehensible words that no one could really believe were Corsican or Aveyronnais.

As time went by, his illness worsened, and he retreated into almost total silence. The visits, following one upon another by the dozens, tended to excite the ordinarily calm Mangin, and he cooperated less and less with the examinations. After the definitive diagnosis of Professor Claude (dementia praecox with negativist attributes), the Ministry of Pensions realized that it was pointless to submit the patient to these meetings with families who thought they recognized him. Mangin would not have altered his indifference even if his true family had turned up at Rodez. For everything else these investigations required—the examination for particular traits, for example—Fenayrou could accomplish the job on his own, without troubling the patient so much. On December 21, 1928, the Ministry of Pensions informed the director of the asylum that it would authorize no further visits, except for special approvals in limited and disputed cases: "Your lodger will thus be protected from trials that—given his mental condition—appear useless and are not without consequence for his health."

Before that restriction was issued, many of those who had initially affirmed that Mangin was their son, husband, or brother withdrew their assurances during the examination, when they could observe the absence of marks that would have been visible on their own missing person, and Fenayrou, always more skeptical than any other skeptic, encouraged them to do so. On only two occasions was the asylum director shaken by a visitor's conviction. The first was a visit from Roger Granger, who had come to find his brother Fernand, a man who resembled Mangin trait for trait. For the first time, it was Fenayrou who was amazed: "I was immediately taken by the resemblance." But in the report he wrote for the prefect the next day, his cool reasoning returned, and he decided the resemblance was insufficient proof: "I wondered, and I am still wondering, whether M. Granger wasn't misled by this resemblance and whether he didn't take a complete stranger for his brother."[48] For the asylum director, resemblances were of little importance; what mattered was that there be no difference at all, not in the slightest detail. It was just this accumulation of details that led Professor Sorel to reject Granger's request for his evaluation on October 24, 1926.[49] The following year, with Lucie Lemay—to whom we shall return—Fenayrou was shaken again.

On the other hand, there were families who could not make up their minds, and who, thinking it over during their trip home, ended up swallowing the dissimilarities with their relative in order to convince themselves, and writing once again to Rodez to categorically affirm their rights. In doing so, they made themselves a party to the denial of death and grieving. From then on they would put all their energy into the lost cause of obtaining Mangin's guardianship. These families, in refusing to face reality, kept alive not only their ordeal but also the tragedy of Anthelme Mangin.

Chapter Five

Against All the Odds:
Three Accounts of Grief

"I can't stop thinking about him. I want so much for him to be mine, because he's all I live for. I think about him all the time."[1] This doleful 1924 letter from Mme. Delafouilhousse, whose claim Professor Sorel had rejected the year before, demonstrated not only how harshly the pain continued but also how hard it was to be rational after having nourished such hopes. She was not the only claimant to continue corresponding with Fenayrou long after he had dispelled her illusions. He answered her with patience and compassion, having come to understand something about suffering; it pained him to observe that material proof counted for little beside such deep emotion.

A Mme. Lallement, "an unhappy mother who comes to him begging him to take an interest in her wretchedness," wrote to the president of the Republic as a last resort. Like others, she insisted that the amnesiac had recognized her and kissed her, and, like others, she brushed aside all counterarguments: "Let the man I believe to be my son out of this dungeon where he's been shut up for ten years so that I can offer him some tenderness. He is so ill! Or else prove to me that he isn't mine."[2] Fenayrou had given her proof—Mangin's head was four centimeters smaller than her missing son's. But any proof that might destroy her last hope was intolerable and, therefore, inadmissible. In just the same way, three mothers named Brille, Mazat, and Mangin refused, against all the odds, to accept the truth, thus complicating a case already tangled in legal actions and all sorts of other pressures. All three recognized Anthelme Mangin as their son in 1922, and all three would carry their claims to the Rodez and Montpellier courts of justice.

On March 26, 1922, hardly a month after it was reported that a man who had gone missing in the Great War was alive and interned in Rodez, the parents of Victor Brille went to the Aveyron departmental asylum. On their return home, they spoke to *Le Petit Journal,* which was pleased to report to its readers that "a missing man from the war has been recognized in Rodez." If they were honest enough "not to be able to claim" that their son had recovered his memory on seeing them, they were all the readier to take offense that their child, who was merely an amnesiac, could be treated as a madman and "incarcerated" in an asylum. The paper offered the mother's account:

> We were received by the director, who had us come into his office. After a lot of dillydallying, he finally consented to send for the boarder we presumed was our son. Once he

came in I had no hesitation. A mother doesn't make mistakes. It was my son, but in what a state! I won't go into it. You can just imagine. His torso was in a kind of straitjacket, and his arms were tied. Why? He didn't seem to be threatening.

To be even more certain of his identity, I asked to see two scars on his arms—one on the left arm from a childhood wound, the other on the right from a shrapnel wound he was treated for before returning to the front. . . . They undressed him. The two scars were clearly visible. Therefore there was no more doubt. I was in the presence of my dear vanished son. . . .

We were left alone with him, my husband and me, for more than an hour. I asked him his name. Immediately he told me his Christian names—Victor Alfred—but added, Mangin. We didn't talk about the reason for this last name.

But he reminded me that before the war he'd lived in the Faubourg Montmartre, and, as I had two umbrellas in my hand, he recognized the one with a steel handle that he had used before leaving for his regiment.[3]

The newspaper account ended by wishing Victor Brille a speedy return to his family, with Deputy Henry Fougère and Professor Gosset of the Salpêtrière Hospital congratulating the happy parents miraculously rescued from their grief. The story would have been happy indeed if it had been true. It was not.

Fenayrou was furious when he learned of the article, especially since he had been accused of treating the amnesiac cruelly. Was the straitjacket the journalist's invention? Whatever the answer, the Brilles said nothing to contradict the *Petit Journal* article. Although Dr. Philippe Pinel, the founder of

French psychiatry, had ordered irons removed from patients and banished similar brutalities at the beginning of the nineteenth century, conditions and patient treatment in insane asylums left a great deal to be desired in the period between the two wars. Straitjackets and coercion, although increasingly criticized since the turn of the century, were still in frequent use.[4] Albert Londres spoke out forcefully against them in his 1925 study, *Chez les fous* (*At the Madhouse*), comparing asylums to prisons and the psychiatrists in charge to wardens: "Three-quarters of the asylums are prehistoric, with alarmingly backward nurses, and rough handling goes on every day."[5] In short, "Madhouses create madmen."[6]

The Rodez facility was not among the most modern. The "open wards" created in Paris by Dr. Edouard Toulouse, which ushered in the modern era in psychiatric hospitals,[7] had not made their way to Rodez—far from it. Overcrowded and decrepit, the asylum had some open land in nearby Cayssiols, but there was nothing to distract or occupy the patients when it rained. Not until December 1935 did the asylum acquire a radio, a movie projector, a billiard table, dominos, playing cards, and checkers and backgammon sets.[8] Until then it made little effort to treat patients humanely, buckling them down and stacking them up rather than attempting to heal them. Mangin, however, was treated differently: he was lodged in a comfortable, well-aired room—partly in deference to his status as the asylum's most famous patient, but to a greater degree as treatment for the beginnings of tuberculosis, which Fenayrou had diagnosed upon the amnesiac's arrival. Harsh treatment was in any case unnecessary for him, given his sweet and submissive character. The straitjacket was pure fantasy.

On April 6, the day after the Brille interview appeared, Fenayrou responded to its charges in a report to the prefect. Nothing, he wrote, had happened the way it was described in *Le Petit Journal*. Before sending for Mangin, he had inquired as to Victor Brille's physical particulars: five foot six, with a shrapnel scar on his right arm and another scar on his left wrist. The examination revealed that the first scar was absent and the second too big to be Victor's. The Brilles had hesitated, and they had left undecided about the amnesiac's identity, although they had noted his strong resemblance to Victor, as well as his interest in their umbrella, which was the very one their son had preferred before the war. Indeed, Fenayrou acknowledged, he had touched it and examined it—but "in the way that he touches and examines everything that is brought to him, such as the buttons on the clothes of those visiting him, the collars of their overcoats, the photos, brochures, letters, etc. . . . ." Fenayrou insisted that he had never left the Brilles alone with the patient, and even if the amnesiac had pronounced the name and address of Victor Brille, his responses supplied no proof of anything, since they could well have been suggested by the visitors themselves. Finally, Fenayrou protested the idea of the straitjacket: "Mangin has been very calm and has never, since he has been in the asylum, manifested violent tendencies." He asked for an inquest to establish the falsehood of the statements attributed to the Brilles, and he demanded an official retraction by the paper regarding the more serious question of recognition, since without one the article might prevent Mangin's true family from stepping forward. For the first time, Fenayrou found out how the activities of the press could damage the process of identification. He also learned, painfully, how relatives of a missing person could vilify him simply because he had found too many discrepancies in their identification. And this was only the beginning.

The local and regional press were the fastest to react. On April 9, *Le Courrier de l'Aveyron* came to the defense of "the likable, welcoming asylum director," demanding, "How could anyone imagine him putting before them the spectacle of a patient confined in a straitjacket, with his arms shackled? . . . Dr. Fenayrou's competence, devotion, and goodness are too well known for us to have to point this out."[9] On April 10, *L'Union catholique* added its voice to the *Courrier*'s.[10] On April 16, the *Journal de l'Aveyron* also took up the asylum director's cause.[11] Pointing out that the Brilles were not the only relatives to have thought they recognized Mangin—Louise Vayssettes had identified the amnesiac as her brother—the weekly went beyond the protests of the other papers to ponder the eventual resolution of the affair, now, in its view, compromised by the assertions of relatives who were as confused as they were convinced.

Jean Grillon, the Aveyron prefect, firmly supported Fenayrou. He wrote to the Ministries of Pensions and of Health to ask for an official denial, adding that on the several occasions he had visited the amnesiac, accompanied by the secretary of the prefecture or Senator Monsservin, Mangin was always calm and docile.[12] Minister Paul Strauss received his request favorably; nevertheless, *Le Petit Journal* did not publish a retraction.

On June 9, Fenayrou learned how deep the Brilles' self-persuasion went. They had contacted the major who dealt with administrative matters in Victor Brille's former regiment, entreating him to cancel their son's death certificate, since he was now interned in Rodez. The major in turn contacted Fenayrou asking for advice, since Victor Brille, as he told the doctor, was not missing but quite dead, killed in battle on December 22, 1915, and buried in the La Motte cemetery, section B, ninth row. The Brilles therefore represented a case of pathological denial. They had learned of their son's death from a comrade on leave, who had brought them his watch, his billfold, his military I.D., and several letters.[13] Nevertheless, the Brilles moved again to assert their views, complaining to the prefecture about the delay in Mangin's transfer to Paris after their recognizing him; and they recruited their son's fiancée to confirm their conviction. On August 3, she wrote a tender letter to Fenayrou in which she asked for news of Victor and to inquire after his health and as to whether "one day he would return to his senses." The asylum director was not opposed to her coming to Rodez, but he assured her that Mangin was certainly not Victor Brille.[14] She wrote back with bitter accusations, persuaded that his maneuvers had been hostile. By this time Fenayrou was thoroughly fed up with the Brilles. He asked the supervisor of disputes at the Ministry of Pensions to deny them permission for further visits to Rodez, which Pensions did on August 21. But no one was counting on the parents' furious determination. With a recommendation from Deputy Fougère, they easily obtained new authorization to visit Anthelme Mangin.

On January 21, 1923, they arrived in Rodez, accompanied by Victor's uncle. This second meeting required them to intensify their denial of the material evidence as well as their denunciation of the director's Machiavellian behavior. Mangin was an inch and a half shorter than Victor Brille? Of course he was: suffering, deprivation, and mental illness had taken their toll on his prewar height. The uncle, when he was interrogated later by an officer from the police prefecture, went so far as to maintain that Mangin's height was five foot four and a half on the side with the broken leg, and five foot six on the good side. Everything was ascribed to Fenayrou's machinations—"I find that this civil servant has shown us a great deal of bad will."[15] But on this second visit, Mangin's right arm was again examined, and once again it showed no evidence of the slightest scar.

> They noticed the absence [Fenayrou wrote in his report] but explained it by saying that the scar had existed but we had found a way to make it vanish. . . . At one point I was assailed by Mme. Brille, who wanted to know what had happened to the scabbed-over black mark that their son had previously had on the bridge of his nose. She said that this mark, still quite visible on Mangin last year, came from a piece of shrapnel that had entered his upper lip a little to the left of center. When I averred that I had never seen this mark on the patient, M. and Mme. Brille maintained that I was

not telling the truth and insinuated that I had caused its disappearance in order to keep Mangin from being recognized as their son.[16]

At the end of the meeting, as Fenayrou persisted in his skepticism, the parents exploded. The mother threatened to go to the president of the Republic, to have the patient removed by force, and, finally, to call "the scandal sheets. . . . They are only waiting for word from me, and it won't cost me a cent."[17] Burning their bridges this way was probably not their best strategy, since their subsequent letter to Senator Monsservin, entreating him to be so kind as to accelerate Mangin's transfer to Paris, was poorly received.[18] So, too, was Deputy Fougère's letter to the Aveyron prefect in support, once again, of the Brilles' cause, which he still considered legitimate.[19]

Definitively rejected by Professor Sorel in his expert evaluation of June 10, 1923, the Brilles refused to give up. On June 19, 1924, they solicited Henry Fougère, who had energetically supported them without fully comprehending the situation, one last time. On that day, in the Chamber of Deputies, he presented a question in writing to the Minister of Pensions: Why had his ministry been so slow in responding to the request that had followed the Brilles' recognition of their son? The reply, which came on July 30, was final:

It has been established that there is no relationship between the lunatic in question and the son of this family. It has furthermore been established that the family's son was killed in armed conflict in December 1915. The family received official notification on January 18 and March 3, 1916. . . . Finally, on June 1, 1921, the family was advised of his temporary burial site and, in July 1923, of the permanent burial site of the deceased soldier. The claim of this family is therefore unfounded.[20]

In losing the support of Deputy Fougère, the Brilles lost their last protector. Thereafter they tried a few grotesque maneuvers that were quickly exposed. In August 1925, Fenayrou compared a request for information from a woman named Arrouet, in Deux-Sèvres, with one from someone named Arrouas that had come the previous July, and discovered that the handwriting belonged to Victor Brille's fiancée, trying to slip past the official barriers in order to get authorization for a visit. But the Brilles could no longer officially claim Mangin, nor even visit him. They would nevertheless go on believing that it was their Victor down there in Rodez, alive, and that no one wanted them to have him.

Strangely enough, Marthe Mazat won the public's heart. Unlike the Brilles, she was neither litigious nor hysterical. All the newspapers spoke of her as the good Mme. Mazat, a little old lady who had left her farm in Dordogne to go live in Rodez near Henri, her missing but now located son. It was once again Paul Bringuier, with his talent for literary invention, who set the tone, describing a sweet and placid octogenarian living in poverty in Rodez, depriving herself of everything in order to spoil her Henri, and peacefully kissing Mangin "without questioning him, without bothering him. . . . To keep from tormenting him she says little to him. She stays near him as long as is permitted and offers him her beautiful old woman's smile. In moments of exaltation she squeezes his arm a little and says to him, in a hushed voice, 'My little one!'"[21] Once again, the truth lay elsewhere.

The Mazats had never accepted the disappearance of their son; they had been trying to find traces of him since 1915. Neither the office of information at the Ministry of War nor the International Red Cross nor the king of Spain[22] was able to help them, so they took up the investigation on their own, seeking out his comrades, his officers, and, once the war was over, German hospitals. They went everywhere in France, from Nice to the Invalides in Paris.[23] Combing asylums and hospitals for a tall, shell-shocked man who might be their son, they found him at last in the Vauclaire asylum, in Dordogne, in the person of a crazed veteran named Laguérie—who promptly died. What a surprise, then, for them to discover a photograph of their son a few months later, this time in Anthelme Mangin. The Rodez amnesiac was therefore only one stage in their fixation, one station of their cross, one step in their denial of death and in their refusal to mourn.

After the photograph of Mangin appeared, these modest peasants from Dordogne asked the Republican Association of Veterans, in Bergerac, to serve as their intermediary. They soon traveled to Rodez in the company of two of Henri Mazat's intimates: Haudeville, who had worked with him in a shoe factory before the war, and Vergnot, a gym teacher. As usual, Fenayrou submitted them all to detailed questioning before bringing the patient in. In particular he noted their

mention of a scar on his scalp; of spots with protruding hairs
on his left cheek, his neck, his chest, and his waist; of a scar
on the groin; of frequent cracking noises made by his right
shoulder; and, finally, affirming Mangin's official description,
a scar on his left wrist and traces of a shovel wound to his
right leg. Fenayrou found the meeting pathetic. Marthe Mazat
saw a fold of skin on the groin as the scar they had mentioned.[24]
He tried to argue, but she would brook no contradiction: the
parents had decided that Mangin was their son—and they
had surely done so before the amnesiac appeared. The most
astonishing aspect of the meeting was that the two comrades
went along with the two old parents, as if caught up in their
enthusiasm or in the ambient madness. A few days later,
Haudeville wrote to the Minister of Pensions to complain
that Fenayrou had been ostentatious in the way he directed
his ill will toward them.[25]

As a result, Fenayrou was obliged once again to justify himself, to point out that he had no reason to doubt the sincerity of
those seeking his assistance but that his job was to take note of
their statements, and that when he refused to see a scar it was
because it did not exist.[26] Asked again the following February
about the meeting, Fenayrou drove his point home:

> Scars such as the one that Mazat had could not have van-
> ished, spots with protruding hairs could not have disap-
> peared without leaving a trace, and the presence of cracking
> sounds in Mangin's right shoulder cannot, in these condi-
> tions, suffice to demonstrate that the patient and M. Mazat
> are one and the same person. I also pointed out to M. and

Mme. Mazat that since they had seen their son in the Vauclaire asylum last year, Mangin must be a stranger to them,
since he was in the Rodez asylum at the time.[27]

The Mazats' version of the meeting was completely different,
and the daily *La Dépêche* was the first to hear about it—in return for which the newspaper fully supported the couple. Some
years later, on September 12, 1933, Joseph Puech informed his
readers that Mangin, when questioned, had recognized his family and his friends: "I recognize all of you," he had said, adding
to his mother, "You are my mommy." The asylum director, who
had noted all the identifying physical characteristics, including
the famous scar on the groin, offered no argument—"It must
have been a miracle that happened in my office."[28] During another visit from Marthe Mazat, the usually silent Mangin was
reported to have uttered the following words: "I thank you for
coming here to try to take me home, but they have sworn that I
will never go home. I thank you all the same, with all my
heart."[29]

Fenayrou, aware of the claims they were making, limited
himself to the hypothesis that they had fallen prey to an illusion, a faulty interpretation of some words the amnesiac had
mumbled.[30] In fact, it was an illusion shared by all the relatives who claimed to recognize Mangin. For example, after
Louise Vayssettes's first encounter with the unknown man,
she was convinced he had declared, "It's incredible, it's obvious, I am Mazenc of the town of Sauveterre."[31]

Unfortunately for the Mazats, and despite the pseudo-
recognition by Mangin, Professor Sorel, the expert who

evaluated the cases of the nine different families, had no difficulty rejecting them all. From the nonexistent scars on Mangin's body, he concluded that the amnesiac was not Henri
Mazat, who had disappeared in Souchez on October 23, 1915,
at the age of thirty-two. For the Mazats, his opinion meant
nothing. They immediately demanded a new evaluation by an
expert they had chosen and who had their confidence: Dr.
Gouzaud, the mayor of Palayrac, their town.[32] The Ministry of
Pensions refused absolutely. The mayor of Palayrac's attempt to
intervene with Fenayrou, pleading for the consolation of "a
mother's broken heart,"[33] was no more successful than Marthe
Mazat's attempt to convince the prefect that the expert Sorel
had been mistaken.[34] To advance their cause, the Mazats col-
lected twenty-four signatures in Gensac, where their son had
lived, and thirty-one in Pessac, where he had worked. All the
signatories, including the mayors of the two towns, recognized
Mazat when presented with the photograph. The petition,
however, did not impress the ever rational Fenayrou, who
countered, "No matter how numerous and certain [the signato-
ries] might be, they cannot alter the decision, which was based
principally on the findings of Professor Sorel."[35]

Undiscouraged, the Mazats traveled regularly to Rodez to
visit Mangin. Fenayrou, always understanding when it came
to the suffering of the families, saw nothing problematic in
their visits, which he authorized. After the death of M. Mazat,
on January 27, 1924, his widow increased her round trips between Palayrac and Rodez. Finally, in July 1925, she moved to
rue Laumière in Rodez, to be near her only child. Fenayrou
could not find it in himself to refuse her permission to visit

twice a week, as he had already granted this to Louise Vays-settes. From then on, Mangin had two mothers in Rodez.

And Marthe Mazat did not leave the situation at that. Having always refused her son's pension—which would have meant acknowledging his death—in December 1924 she undertook legal action to cancel his death certificate. But after the Rodez court, on July 30, 1930, declared itself unauthorized to rule on the case, she made a claim against the Ministry of Pensions in the same court on April 16, 1931.[36] That particular case never progressed any further, but Marthe Mazat figured among the last families in litigation, from 1935 to 1939.

It all began on August 1, 1922, the day the widow Mangin, accompanied by her daughter, went to Rodez and instantly recognized the patient presented to her. But the case of the woman from Nantes was even more untenable than those of the Brilles and the Mazats. In fact, Roger Mangin, inducted in 1918, had gone missing the night of May 26–27, 1918, near Soissons. By that date the living unknown soldier was already interned in the Clermont-Ferrand asylum, and so the two men could not be confused; it was pointless to dwell on the scar on Roger Mangin's forehead that the Rodez amnesiac did not have, or on his height of five feet six and a half inches, or on his youth—he would have been twenty-two in 1922, when the patient in the Aveyron asylum appeared to be thirty. In spite of all the evidence, Mme. Mangin insisted, coming up with a hypothesis that turned into a conviction she would never abandon: that a mistake had been made at the Bron or the Clermont-Ferrand asylum, an unfortunate mix-up between two patients, and it had victimized her, the legitimate mother. Her son had not been repatriated on February 1, 1918, but in 1919. And from the beginning she ensnared Fenayrou in her irrationality.

No argument is strong enough to win the confidence of those afflicted with the "grieving syndrome,"[37] as Carine Trévisan has called it. All facts are brushed aside or reconstituted to fit the sufferer's desires. The director tried to reason with the widow Mangin, and for his efforts to penetrate her delirium, he was scorned, despised, and eventually calumniated as an underhanded manipulator who just wanted to place the amnesiac with another family. Thus the putative mistake in dates, from 1918 to 1919, became in her mind a deliberate falsification by Fenayrou.

In November 1922, Deputy Réné Delafoy of the Loire-Inférieure department was taken in by the mother's grief, as Fougère was by the Brilles' at about the same time. Promoting Mme. Mangin's thesis before the ministers of war and pensions, Delafoy suggested that a mistake in dates could have occurred. After all, hadn't the patient himself pronounced his first and last names in the presence of the doctor? And hadn't Mme. Mangin received a letter and a card from her son, providing ample proof of his identity?[38] Both claims were patently false, but bowing, apparently, to the authority of the deputy, on December 6 the Ministry of Pensions granted his request for a new evaluation of the Mangin file. Fenayrou was contacted, and, feeling stung by the complaints and recriminations the widow Mangin and her daughter had made to the attorney general, he declined any responsibility for the evaluation and refused to designate an expert to conduct it: "Any designation made by me will not fail to be criticized by Mme. Mangin, and these ladies probably will not accept the expert's conclusions if they do not confirm their own statements."[39] Fully aware of how improbable the falsification hypothesis was, Fenayrou knew how this second evaluation would turn out, and he was just as certain that the conclusions would not rein in the Mangins' obsession: "These ladies' conviction is so strong that nothing, it appears, will counter it, and it seems certain they will persevere even if the designated expert declares them in error."[40] He was right. While waiting and worrying about the amnesiac's worsening tuberculosis, Fenayrou nevertheless urged that the evaluation be extended to the claims of the eight other families— the Bettons, Brilles, Ceccaldis, Delafouilhousses, Gastineaus, Mazats, Mazencs, and Rivières—who, despite his own deep skepticism, continued to see their son in Mangin.[41] On February 22, 1923, the Ministry of Pensions put the prefect in charge of the appeal, allowing him the choice of a medical-legal authority from the faculty at Toulouse or of Montpellier and the freedom, then, "to have done with it." On April 17, the dean of the Toulouse faculty of medicine designated Professor Sorel. The evaluation took place on May 5 at 1:30 P.M., in the presence of all nine families. All nine cases would be dismissed.

Even with the facts marshaled against her, the widow Mangin redoubled her efforts to enlighten the authorities about Fenayrou's manipulations. On May 9 she wrote to the minister of the interior:

It is urgent that you know about the odious charade unfolding in this asylum, of which my son is the unfortunate victim. . . .

I assure you that my son won't last a month longer with the atrocious treatment he is receiving. On our first visit, they had bleached his mustache almost blond. M. Expert is certainly not aware of all they have done to disfigure him. . . .

They forbid him to speak or to write. They don't leave him alone with us for one minute.

Fenayrou, denounced again, was not even informed of this last letter. The prefect, a competent, dedicated, principled professional, sent the letter on to the minister of health without thinking it necessary to trouble Fenayrou over "Mme. Mangin's ridiculous and untruthful accusations."[42] The preceding January, the asylum director, growing philosophical, had decided not to concern himself any longer with attacks on his ostensible ill will. "I don't believe I need to focus on the charges made about me by Mme. Mangin," he wrote in a letter, "for whom I have only feelings of pity, because of the wretchedness that the loss of her son has brought her. The prefect understands what her charges are worth, and that is all I need."[43] The prefect had taken note. From then on it was he who replied to inquiries from his superiors regarding complaints from families who claimed to have recognized Mangin.

Since the Brilles' slander, the minister of pensions had been aware of the madness that self-persuasion could nourish. He gave no credence to information that cast suspicion on Fenayrou. On the contrary, he praised him: "I have appreciated the considerateness and the conscientiousness always shown by the director under the circumstances, and I believe that Mangin could not be in better hands."[44] Like his colleague at the Ministry of Pensions, the minister of health spoke of Fenayrou's "high integrity" and "professional conscientiousness."[45] The asylum director also received the unanimous praise of the Aveyron General Council in a session of May 6, 1926. Its president, Senator Monsservin, decried the allegations brought by several newspapers that had failed to verify their sources. The supposed machinations of the asylum director were denounced as "a melodramatic novel in which no one who knew Dr. Fenayrou could believe."[46] All the same, the Aveyron prefect made it clear that he would not be sorry to see the troubling affair removed from his responsibility by getting rid of the amnesiac—that is, by transfering him to another asylum. That was out of the question, the minister of pensions shot back: "The removal of the former soldier Mangin Anthelme from the asylum at Rodez, motivated simply by the fact that accusations have been brought either against your administration or against the asylum administration, would give these accusations more credence than I give them."[47] The uproar, far from embarrassing the Rodez asylum and bringing about Mangin's transfer, had the paradoxical result of anchoring the amnesiac in Aveyron indefinitely.

Thus the request to transfer the unknown man to the asylum at Nantes, formulated by the widow Mangin while she was waiting for her file to be evaluated, was scornfully rejected on June 25, 1923, even though five days earlier the Loire-Inférieure departmental prefect had not only given his accord but also offered to cover the costs of the move. Every new failure reinforced the widow, who, in her martyrdom, was increasingly persuaded of a plot against her. "The resistance I have encountered proves to anyone who doesn't know that I am denied all justice," she railed.[48] The despair of defeat infuriated her, particularly against Louise Vayssettes, who was being allowed two weekly visits with the man that she, for her part, considered *her* brother.[49] But Mme. Mangin's principal target remained the odious Fenayrou. A meeting on August 1 was, she thought, nothing but a maneuver: "It was already decided in the asylum to refuse me my son and to give him to the X family."[50]

Somewhere between a comedy and a tragedy, the affair might have been amusing if Mme. Mangin had not been driven to the point of madness by the loss of her son. Several times a year she sent packages to the amnesiac, along with cards on his birthday—that is, on Roger Mangin's birthday—and she wrote regularly to the Aveyron prefect for news of his health, which Fenayrou willingly transmitted. On August 7, 1927, she went too far and received a warning from the prefect for a passage in a letter in which, referring to Fenayrou, she wrote that she rejected "the illegal manner of his actions." Her later correspondence was no less vehement, and in December 1928 the prefect renewed his threat to stop sending her information about her son's health if she kept up her offensive remarks. Denouncing the "arbitrary sequestration" of her son, she wrote, "I formally refuse to have anything to do with my son's doctor-executioner in order to have news. My son writes French properly. I would like to have a word written in his hand."[51] The idea of her son as a prisoner prevented from writing hounded her. In letters of February 28 and August 20, 1930, she persisted in failing to understand why he did not write her himself—or, rather, she understood all too well.

Madly she continued, mobilizing deputy François Blancho of the Loire-Inférieure department, trying to convince another deputy, Louis Malvy, and assailing the president of the Rodez court with her far-fetched explanations of the flagrant inconsistencies between the physical attributes of Roger Mangin and Anthelme Mangin. Like the Brilles, she explained the decline in his height by the fracture that had shortened the unfortunate soldier's tibia.[52] As for the mistaken dates, she offered some corrections in December 1931: Mangin had not been repatriated in February 1918 but in February 1919, with the last convoy returning amnesiac prisoners from Germany to France.[53] This sleight-of-hand did not help. Then she decided that if Fenayrou wanted to give the amnesiac to another family, it must be because they were paying him; and thus every claimant family became suspect to her. Indeed, how could they, in good faith, seek the guardianship of Anthelme Mangin when she alone was his mother? Obviously the other families were lying and motivated by money—for in 1920 Mangin had been reclassified, entitling him to an invalid's 100 percent pension, though he could not actually collect it as long as his identity remained undetermined, since pensions are issued only to identified persons. The money coming to him eventually piled up into a tidy sum, a factor that, if the newspapers were to be believed, excited greed—though the newspapers clearly understood nothing about the dilemma of mourning the missing.

Mangin's nest egg was estimated at 60,000 francs by *L'Union catholique* in February 1926[54] and at 200,000 francs by *L'Intransigeant* in 1935.[55] In fact, both figures were exaggerated. *Le Petit Parisien,* having done the math, challenged the sum reported by *L'Union catholique:* in 1926 the amnesiac's pension would have been not *60,000* francs but only *20,000,* and, subtracting the cost of his stay at the asylum (7 francs a day), there would have been only about 6,000 francs left for Mangin and his family[56]—far from the fortune reported, though it was sufficient to sustain the paranoia, including the paranoia at the Ministry of Pensions.[57] Whatever the true figure was, Mangin's fantasy pension formed the basis of hypotheses about criminal behavior that accounted both for being pushed aside and for the bad faith of the other hopeful families. For everyone always had the same explanation— the suspicion of greedy motives was pervasive, but good faith was always considered unique. This was why Mme. Mangin did not give up and continued hoping to make the diabolical process fail, repeating with everyone else that there were only two kinds of families, "those that substitute him for another man to get the money and us, his real family, who oppose his sequestration."[58]

Deep in her delirium, Mme. Mangin believed she had formal proof establishing the identity of her son. "Everything has been proved . . . the trial has been won," she assured the dumbfounded prefect on February 13, 1931. And, four years later: "I don't doubt that you will put an end to this difficult situation without delay by returning my son to his true family."[59] Receiving no reply—it was pointless to reason with her—she wrote a desolate letter to the prime minister on January 14, 1935, the day the Rodez trial was about to begin. If she was still in the last handful of claimants, she also knew that she had no chance of triumphing, because by then the case was really between only two families, the Lemays and the Monjoins.

Chapter Six

Lemay vs. Monjoin

With the claims made by Lucie Lemay in 1927 and Joseph and Pierre Monjoin in 1930, the case took a new turn. For the first time, the claimants were something other than deluded families demanding the amnesiac despite clear proof that their positions were untenable.

In 1914, Marcel and Lucie Lemay were twenty-five and twenty-two years old, respectively. They were a happy couple and the parents of three children. Marcel Lemay, who worked for a large distributor of mineral water, was a pious, cultivated man with a curious mind. He knew English, was striving to learn German, and had begun studying Latin just before the war. Years later, his family could remember his strong voice shaking the walls of the apartment at 53 rue Defrance in Vincennes.[1] The mobilization interrupted the Lemays' happiness, and the spouses had just time to have photographs made to exchange—he in uniform, smiling and relaxed, she with the children. On August 4, the day before Marcel Lemay's departure for the front, he sent an express letter to his wife:

> My dear little wife,
> Just a word to give you my news. We are overwhelmed with preparations for our departure, which will take place tomorrow, Wednesday. We are all full of courage, confidence, and hope; a word from you would make me happy; you can come see me if you aren't too tired. . . . I kiss you as many times as I can. Pray for me, don't forget me. Kiss the little ones and everybody. Millions of kisses.
> Marcel[2]

This first letter was also his last. Sergeant Marcel Lemay went missing on September 13, 1914, in Loivre, in the department of Marne, ten kilometers northwest of Reims. The information form from his outfit turned up in the army archives.[3] At the time he went missing, he was presumed to have been taken prisoner, and the prisoner lists exchanged by the warring nations confirmed this presumption: Lemay was interned in the Senne camp in Westphalia. Lucie, who had received no news, wrote the Red Cross, which told her that as of November 20 her husband was alive and imprisoned at Senne. But the packages she sent him were all marked "unknown" and returned, and none of the subsequent searches offered any further confirmation of her husband's existence.[4]

On August 7, 1915, her hopes were rekindled when she thought she recognized Marcel in a photograph in *L'Illustration* that came from a report on the arrival of the first convoy of repatriates in France.[5] Among the gravely wounded, the amputees, the blind, the paralyzed, and the demented, all of them welcomed back as heroes in the Lyon railway station, she identified her husband, a cigarette in his mouth, in the second row. The resemblance was confirmed by his sister and several other people who had known him well. But when nothing corroborated her hope, she had to assume that she had been the victim of an illusion. The wait went on, and like many others plunged into silence, she wished impatiently for the war to end: "I thought that the Germans had locked him in a fortress, and that he would come back to me after the war, but, alas, the waiting went on and, seeing prisoners returned to their families, I lost all hope."[6] Human error may have been the source of her ordeal: while Sergeant Lemay's registration papers indicated he was shot down in Loivre, in the department of Marne, the Red Cross indicated that he had been taken prisoner in Guise, in the department of Aisne.[7] This inconsistency remains a mystery, but in any case Marcel Lemay never returned from the war, and on October 5, 1923, the Paris court declared his wife a widow.

At that time, Lucie Lemay had been living in Coulonges-sur-Autize in the department of Deux-Sèvres, where for nine years she had a tobacco store on the place du Château. Having abruptly left Vincennes at the beginning of September 1914, following the German advance, she found refuge in the countryside of Deux-Sèvres, liked it there, and decided to stay. Nothing really was keeping her in Vincennes anyway; moreover, in her absence her apartment there had been pillaged. She lived precariously, doing housework and denying herself in order to raise her children with dignity. In time she fell ill and lost a lung. Her situation improved when she acquired a small business. At the end of 1927, when she was finally getting back a little stability, she found a magazine in her dentist's waiting room with a picture of a man's face that reminded her of her husband's, and she was astonished to read that he was an amnesiac whose identity was unknown. "Right away my grandmother wrote to the proper authorities," Louise Lemay, her granddaughter, reported years later. "Her ordeal began on that day."[8]

Granted permission by the Ministry of Pensions on December 19, 1927, to go to Rodez, she was in the office of the asylum director at ten o'clock the next morning. Unfortunately, while she claimed to recognize her husband in the photographs—even though he was "so much older"—she could not furnish a list of distinguishing characteristics to Fenayrou. "She told me that even though she had imagined that it might be useful one day," the doctor noted in his report to the prefect, "she had never written down a description of her husband or thought up anatomical or other peculiarities that might help later in his identification."[9] She spoke more confidingly to Professor Sorel, invoking her and her husband's modesty to explain her lack of knowledge about any scars or marks on the skin that Marcel Lemay might have.[10] When Mangin was presented to her, she immediately declared that he was her husband, displaying great emotion and, like others before her, proffering tender caresses, sweet words, and a flood of memories. She showed him photographs of his now grown children. But, as usual, Mangin was indifferent. He limited himself to touching the collar of Lucie Lemay's jacket several times and trying her hat on, backward. The hardest part for her was his failure to recognize her. In their eagerness to claim Mangin as their son or husband, families often convinced themselves that he had recognized them, or at least shown some friendly feeling toward them. Lucie Lemay quickly perceived the impossibility of communicating with him, and she was desolate. "Ah! Yes, it's him, it's most certainly him," she said, "but I always believed he would recognize me. It's him. Ah! My God! Ah! I didn't expect to see him so disturbed, not like that. . . . If only he had recognized me."[11]

While the article Jean Aicardi later wrote for *Le Petit Marseillais* faithfully described this meeting, the journalist clearly having had access to Fenayrou's report,[12] Paul Bringuier's continuing soap opera invented freely, reporting that Mangin recognized Mme. Lemay "to please her" and kissed her before she fainted from the shock.[13] This version also made it into the columns of the *Journal* magazine in 1936, where Lucie Lemay, interviewed by Yves Gaël, was reported to have said that at that December 20, 1927, meeting Mangin had taken her head in his hands "like he used to" and kissed her tenderly on the forehead: "I was overwhelmed, so it wasn't surprising that I didn't hear the poor man tell me, 'I recognize you,' even though Dr. Fenayrou immediately noted it in his records."[14] There is no such observation in the Aveyron asylum director's report. It is conceivable that Lucie Lemay, more than eight years after the events, reimagined the meeting as she would have liked it to happen—unless the journalist invented his own "interview" on the basis of a few sparse articles, without even going to Coulonges-sur-Autize to speak to her.

Still, if Mangin had been indifferent during her visit, Fenay-rou was touched by the emotion she showed and said that he was "deeply impressed." Never before, he went on, had any declaration of recognition concerning Mangin been based on such a strong similarity in official descriptions. The color of the eyes, the hair, the shape of the face, the height, the approximate age of the amnesiac—everything matched. Or rather almost everything, because Mangin, unlike Marcel Lemay, didn't know a word of German or of Latin. That might appear to be only a slight discrepancy, but Fenayrou was not a man to rely on mere similarities. For Mangin to be placed with a family de-finitively, there had to be no doubt. He reiterated his theory to the prefect on February 28, 1928: "It appears once again that it's not only in looking for and finding more or less numerous points of resemblance that we will be able to establish a con-nection between Mangin and someone else with certainty; this connection cannot be considered proved unless there exists no point of dissimilarity." Accordingly, Fenayrou had asked for Professor Sorel's evaluation before giving his opinion.

The pace of the government was not the pace of the fami-lies. Lucie Lemay, impatient with the slowness of the investi-gation, wrote to the minister of pensions and to Senator Duteau several times. In February 1928, unable to bide her time any longer, she returned to Rodez, where she remained for several days, hoping to have the patient turned over to her then and there. This second visit went worse than the first. Having thought about the matter since the December meeting, Mme. Lemay could come up with only two distinctive traits: a deformed knee with a bone spur, and an abscess behind the outside ankle that had been removed in February 1914. On Sunday, February 12, she saw Mangin, who was ill and in bed: "His attitude toward his visitor was immediately hostile," Fenayrou reported, "and he showed an unmistakable impatience for her to leave. The following days he was more sociable but still indifferent. The fact that he twice went to sleep during a visit, in spite of all the affection he was getting, indicates his lack of interest in Mme. Lemay's company."[15] On February 15, in Lucie Lemay's presence, Fenayrou looked for the deformed knee and the scar in the ankle region; he found nothing. Doubts began to accumulate, and with renewed caution he once again asked Sorel's advice. His doubts were confirmed a few days later when he received the letter that Lucie Lemay had sent to the minister of pensions on January 31. Protesting the delay in winning her case, she had written that when she was there Mangin had recalled "some memory from his past," that she had succeeded in making him speak, and that he remembered Paris. Asked about this assertion, Fenayrou denied it completely: "Like many before her, Mme. Lemay, totally convinced of having found her husband in Mangin, is apt to retain from what she sees or hears only what will support her position. She has, on the other hand, a tendency to reject as valueless . . . elements that discredit her position."[16]

Professor Sorel's evaluation took place on April 22, 1928, in the presence of Lucie Lemay, who had once again made the trip to Rodez. Sorel described her as "a nice-looking woman who appears sincere and whom no argument can budge."[17] Sorel could explain no better than Fenayrou why the patient, if he was Marcel Lemay, did not know German or Latin and

ABOVE: The first published photograph of the amnesiac of Rodez, Bron asylum, 1918. (Jean-Yves Le Naour)

Years later, at the asylum in Vaucluse. (Jean-Yves Le Naour)

LES MILITAIRES FRAPPÉS D'AMNÉSIE

Il y a quelque temps, le 23 décembre, exactement, le *Petit Parisien* informait ses lecteurs qu'il existait encore dans les hôpitaux des soldats frappés d'amnésie et dont on ignore l'identité. A la suite de cet article, nous avons reçu nombre de lettres : des parents dont le fils a disparu au cours de la guerre nous demandaient de publier les photographies de ces malheureux inconnus. Nous avons pu nous procurer le document, qui est affiché dans les bureaux de la place de Paris et dans un certain nombre de centres régionaux.

Ce document reproduit les traits et le signalement de dix militaires non identifiés, mais sur lesquels quatre sont morts à l'heure actuelle. Nous ne publions donc que les portraits des six survivants, dans l'espoir que cette publication servira à les faire reconnaître par ceux qui peuvent encore s'intéresser à leur sort — et qu'elle évitera en tout cas de faire se prolonger davantage de pénibles incertitudes et de douloureuses illusions.

GUEGAUD (?) Clément
Rapatrié d'Allemagne, asile de Saint-Pons (Nice). Cicatrice rectiligne au sourcil gauche. Tatouages sur le bras droit.

(?)
A l'asile de Bron. Age 27 ou 28 ans, cheveux châtains, yeux gris, sourcils bruns très épais. Taille : 1 68. Bonne dentition. Accent méridional très prononcé.

IGNACE (?)
Serbe, dont le nom serait Glavko (?). Entré à l'asile de Bron le 31 juillet 1917.

BERRINET (?)
Entré à l'asile de Bron le 1er février 1918. Taille : 1m57, yeux bleus, cheveux châtain clair, barbe blonde. Ni cicatrices, ni tatouages.

HALUIN ou ELUIN (?) Frédéric
Il parle de Mouchy-la-Cache, près d'Authies-Péronne. Taille 1m53, cheveux et sourcils châtains, front découvert, yeux gris-bleu, nez fin. Cicatrices de brûlures. Parle avec difficulté.

MANGIN (?) (Anthelme)
Asile d'aliénés de Clermont-Ferrand, vient de l'asile de Bron. Taille : 1m66, yeux châtains ; cheveux châtains foncés clairsemés, barbe châtaine, teint pâle.

Six amnesiac soldiers, revealed by *Le Petit Parisien*, January 10, 1920, so that "our publication might keep painful uncertainties and disappointments from being prolonged." Anthelme Mangin is in the bottom right corner. (*Le Petit Parisien*)

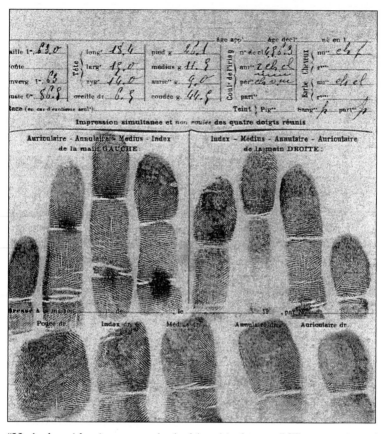

"He had no identity papers, he had lost his dog tag." The amnesiac of Rodez's fingerprints. (Jean-Yves Le Naour)

"The dead come back from the war." Frans Masereel's depiction of the unknown soldiers. (Kharbine-Tapabor/ADAGP)

LEFT: One soldier, many families. The illustration accompanied Paul Bringuier's May 15, 1935, article in *L'Intransigeant*.

BELOW: "He's my son! He's my husband! He's my brother!" Anthelme Mangin appears on the cover of *Detective*, January 21, 1937.

L'intransigeant's 1934 depiction of wives, mothers, and daughters with Anthelme Mangin, searching for signs of recognition. (Jean-Yves Le Naour)

Madame Mazat with a photograph of the son she believed had come back from the front as the amnesiac of Rodez. (Jean-Yves Le Naour)

LEFT: Marcel Lemay, 1914. (Lemay family)

BELOW: Lucie Lemay with her children, 1914. (Lemay family)

Octave Felicien Monjoin, circa 1914. (Jean-Yves Le Naour)

Joseph Monjoin at his parents' home, *Paris Soir*, January 31, 1935. (*Paris Soir*)

RIGHT: Anthelme Mangin at Vaucluse. (Jean Yves-Le Naour)

BELOW: Anthelme Mangin's funeral, April 4, 1948. (Jean-Yves Le Naour)

showed no trace of the scar where the abscess had been excised, not to mention the deformed knee: "All in all, if certain descriptive details, such as height, apparent age, color of hair, eyebrows, mustache, are common to both Marcel Lemay and Mangin, more important attributes are not. . . . None of Marcel Lemay's characteristic traits are the same as Mangin's; no physical anomaly of Mangin's exists on Lemay. I don't believe these two people are one and the same."[18]

Like all the other convinced claimants who had preceded her, Lucie Lemay refused to give up with Sorel's report. Mangin's old injury puzzled her; having no knowledge that her husband had had a fractured right leg, she wrote to the veterans' associations. On May 12, 1928, *La Voix du combattant* launched an appeal to its readers: Would all those who knew Sergeant Marcel Lemay, in the 28th Regiment or in the Senne camp, please come forward in order to help his wife learn about his wound and his disappearance?[19] On May 19, the journal reported that it was pleased to be able to offer several comrades ready to identify Lemay, and it requested the transfer of Mangin to Paris, near his old home and his former friends and coworkers, in order to facilitate the identification.[20] One Langlois, who had been a prisoner in the Senne camp, claimed to remember Lemay in captivity with a broken leg, because he had walked with crutches.[21]

Lemay's former boss, a M. Foucault, the dealer in mineral water, also answered the journal and Lucie Lemay's appeal. He did not want to remain silent, but neither was he sure of the facts, given that in 1914 he had had more than a hundred employees.[22] He nevertheless traveled to Rodez on August 24 and gave Mangin a dictation test on different types of mineral water. Mangin wrote down a number of them correctly: for example, for Vichy Grande Grille he wrote "Vichy Gde Grille," as in the company's catalog. But there were also mistakes: rue Curial, the address of the Foucault business, he wrote down as "rue Kurial"; and he transformed Fontaine-Bonneleau into "fontaine Bonne l'o" and Couzan-Brault into "Couzan-Bro." Despite these few errors, Lemay's old boss was impressed. He softened his earlier skepticism, saying that he could "no longer affirm that Mangin and Lemay were two different people."[23] Lucie Lemay was delighted: according to her, if Mangin had pronounced the word *Vichy* to those interrogating him in February 1918, it was not because that was where he was from—this test had proved it was a memory from his former job.[24] Fenayrou was far less certain. In his view, it was useless to discuss the observations made in this evaluation, the correct or incorrect spelling of this or that word, because Mangin, as Sorel had already established, was not Lemay.[25] Foucault, who had been so supportive in letters to Lucie Lemay on August 30 and September 6, backed down when he learned of Fenayrou's position:

Madame,

I am not convinced that the patient whom I saw at Rodez is your husband.

As I told you, I noted certain things, and I communicated them to the doctor at the asylum, along with a handwriting specimen of Lemay's from 1914. Some time afterward, I received a letter from him telling me that, taking into consideration what I had said and the handwriting of the hospitalized man and numerous other facts, he was certain that the patient wasn't your husband. . . .

Raise your children, since you are lucky enough to be able to do so.[26]

For Lucie Lemay, the disappointment was intense, and Fenayrou's ill will was confirmed. With his opposition, all her efforts were likely to be in vain. Her position was further threatened, beginning in 1930, with the appearance of the Monjoins, a family who advanced evidence so striking that the government found it convincing.

All the other families who went to Rodez thought they recognized their relative in a photograph published in the newspapers. The Monjoins arrived by a completely different route. They had never even known about the Rodez amnesiac; moreover, when Joseph Monjoin was confronted with Mangin, he didn't recognize him—much to the surprise of Fenayrou, who was sure he had finally found the amnesiac's real family. Borges and Pirandello, who respectively in "The Improbable Impostor Tom Castro" and *Right You Are (If You Think You Are)* had written of a desire to believe that goes beyond physical resemblances, would never have imagined that the true relatives might hesitate where so many others had convinced themselves so totally. That, nevertheless, is what happened.

Octave Félicien Monjoin was an independent young man. Born in Saint-Maur-sur-Indre, a village close to Châteauroux, on March 19, 1891, he left his family of modest warehouse-men and laborers early on. In Châteauroux, he began his career as a waiter, remaining there for five years; then he moved around, taking jobs in Tours, Etretat, Monte Carlo, Paris, and, finally, London, where he worked for two years in the Ottoman embassy, as a bellhop and sometimes a cook.[27] He had to return to France for his military service, and went to war as part of the the 95th Regiment at Bourges.[28] On August 18, 1914, he was wounded in Blamont and taken prisoner; he continued to send news until February 1916, then nothing further. No death certificate was drawn up, because officially Octave Monjoin was not dead, and no such declaration was filed by the German authorities. The monument to the dead that faces the Saint-Maur-sur-Indre city hall does not bear his name. When his brother, Joseph, was demobilized, he attempted to get information from the Ministry of War about Octave, who had never come home, but he received no reply. In 1924, if the newspaper *Centre-Éclair* is to be believed, the mayor of Saint-Maur wrote the Ministry of Pensions in the hope that the elderly father, Pierre, might be allowed to receive the pension due the son who had died for France;[29] but the ministry did not reply to him, either—no doubt because Octave Monjoin was not one of the missing whose absence had to be recategorized as death but, rather, a living person who had vanished.

It was thus with the idea of getting a pension for his father and changing his brother's classification for good that Joseph Monjoin wrote to the ministry on May 13, 1930:

I have the honor of forwarding you this request to reclassify the position of my brother, who was taken prisoner at the beginning of the 1914–1918 war, and who has not sent news since the year 1916. . . .

Since then, there has been no further word from him. My father, who is seventy-four years old, never wanted to have anything done to reclassify his position until today.

Now it seems time to bring an end to this false situation and for my father to receive the pension to which he is entitled.[30]

A few days later, the ministry answered him that, according to its records, "it appears that the soldier Monjoin Octave was interned successively in Karlsruhe, Rastadt, Merselburg, Darmstadt, and Hameln, and that he was not reported to be deceased."[31] The authorities had lost track of him in Konstanz after he was liberated. The Bureau of Disputes, which had been handling the Anthelme Mangin affair since 1922, quickly established a connection between Octave Monjoin, present on January 31, 1918, in a convoy of repatriates bound the next day for France, and the unknown soldier discovered wandering the platforms of the Lyon-Brotteaux railway station on February 1. Thus, almost by accident, and without all the commotion stirred up by publicity about the amnesiac having served any purpose, the Ministry of Pensions finally found itself on the right track.

At the end of 1930, the ministry asked Joseph Monjoin to send photographs and samples of his missing brother's handwriting. A picture of Anthelme Mangin accompanied the letter, with the following question: "Do you recognize him?"[32] Joseph did not recognize Mangin, but he still sent Fenayrou the requested items, because the coincidence was disturbing. On November 21, the Aveyron prefect was informed about the soldier Monjoin, "who went missing during his repatriation from Konstanz to Lyon, on January 31, 1918." It was not just the dates and the locales that matched; so did the descriptions of the two men. These conditions called for a handwriting evaluation by the eminent Dr. Locard. The asylum director accordingly dictated to Mangin the text of three postcards that Monjoin had sent to his family as a prisoner. At the last one, when he was asked to write "I'll lay you a good bottle that we're not having much fun here,"[33] the amnesiac expressed "a rather marked nervousness."[34] But the choice of expert posed a problem: Locard had already evaluated Mangin's handwriting and had mistakenly found it identical with the Canadian Rondot's. "It appears, under these circumstances, that asking Locard to undertake a new evaluation would be placing him in a very delicate situation,"[35] the prefect asserted. For this reason they turned to Samaran, an expert connected with the Seine court. Fenayrou, impressed with the case for the Monjoins, asked for a meeting to take place quickly.

On January 14, 1931, Joseph Monjoin was invited, in spite of his misgivings, to meet the Rodez amnesiac. Until then, permissions for visits had been granted in response to requests from families; in the case of the Monjoins, who were merely requesting a pension, the roles were reversed, and they practically had to be begged to attend. By March 6, Fenayrou was growing impatient. Joseph Monjoin had not yet traveled to Rodez nor, in fact, responded at all. When the ministry investigated, Monjoin explained that he could not afford the trip to Rodez, and in an act of generosity, the ministry granted him two hundred francs to cover his expenses and move the process forward.[36]

The meeting between Joseph Monjoin and Anthelme Mangin finally took place at the beginning of April. It was a disappointment. The amnesiac, predictably, maintained his habitual indifference, and his ostensible brother did not really recognize him. "I was very moved," Monjoin told a journalist from the *Progrès de l'Indre* a couple of months later. "I tried to question him, but I got nothing. His voice was not the voice I remembered, but in fifteen years a man changes." And speaking to Jean Aicardi the following September he said, "To tell you the truth, the first impression left me perplexed. This man in front of me was unreacting, motionless, with a lost look; I hardly recognized my brother. Hadn't nearly eighteen years gone by since I'd last seen Félicien?"[37] Later he backed off from his initial reaction, observing that in addition to what the passage of years had wrought, Mangin's mustache had startled him; his brother hadn't had one. Nevertheless, Fenayrou had made up his mind. He gave no more weight to Joseph Monjoin's hesitation than he had to the earlier proclamations of recognition. He was convinced that Mangin and Monjoin were the same person.

For confirmation, he turned once again to the expert Sorel.[38] The evaluation took place on June 6. In the report

Sorel sent to the prefect on June 20, he formally concluded that Monjoin and the amnesiac were one person. He cited the analyses of various specialists, Samaran for graphology, the engineer Mache for anthropometry: "Ultimately all the comparisons, anthropological [*sic*], graphological, photographic, lead us to the conviction that we have finally solved the problem we have been seeking a solution to since 1923: Octave Monjoin is the lunatic who was until this day unidentified. . . . This identification is far more the result of the asylum director's efforts than of mine." When this report reached the supervisor of disputes at the Ministry of Pensions, he decided to seek additional information and launched an investigation in Germany through the Ministry of Foreign Affairs. While awaiting the results, the authorities chose to keep the conclusions of Sorel's report confidential.

They were not altogether successful. Jean Aicardi provided a very well informed account of the solution to the unknown-soldier enigma in *Le Petit Marseillais*. He may have been the first to impart the good news to Joseph Monjoin, whom he met at the beginning of September in Saint-Maur-sur-Indre. His report even had the providential effect of eliciting new testimony: following the articles that appeared between May 21 and May 25, 1931, he had received an enormous amount of mail (including letters from dowsers who were sweeping the map of France with their oscillating pendants), and after his series of articles on September 8 to September 15, he received a letter from one of Monjoin's former comrades in captivity, which he rushed into print on September 22. Emile

THE LIVING UNKNOWN SOLDIER

Lejard remembered Octave Monjoin, with whom he had been held captive at the camp in Hameln, and his progression into dementia. Sweet, docile, sunk in silence, he no longer had any cognizance of his situation, and his comrades even had to remind him to wash himself. Eventually he was transferred into a barracks reserved for the mad. "I saw him, once or twice, through the bars on the windows," Lejard recalled, "with the same look, lost in oblivion. I hadn't heard anything about him since then. Still, I remember very clearly his emaciated face and his curly chestnut hair, as well as his dirty ragged clothes, the tunic with the number from the 95th Regiment. This number was engraved in my memory, because I had a close relative in that regiment stationed in Bourges."[39]

A report about the prisoner Octave Monjoin provided by Germany removed any remaining doubts. It contained the information that Monjoin had been treated for a fracture to the right leg, and that he had been developing dementia praecox:

Monjoin was taken prisoner on August 18, 1914, near Blamont (Meurthe-et-Moselle department). He was treated in the Bavarian hospital of Domene from August 23–25, 1914, for a fracture of the thigh he had incurred by falling from a wall. From there he was taken behind the lines to Blamont, then hospitalized from August 29 to November 9, 1914, in Reserve Hospital No. 5 in Karlsruhe for the fracture of the leg. He was then taken via Rastadt to the camp in Darmstadt, where he belonged to the 5th Battalion of the 19th Company of prisoners. From the Hameln camp (regimental soldier no.

13,391), Monjoin was evacuated to the prisoners' hospital XAK in that town, and from there to the prisoner-of-war camp in Vechta from June 20, 1917, to January 26, 1918, for dementia praecox, and evacuated to France on January 31, 1918, via Konstanz, still not cured.[40]

Faced with such an accumulation of proof, there was no reason left to tarry, and the minister asked his colleague at Justice to officially identify Mangin as Monjoin. Lucie Lemay saw the newspapers that had been supporting her case drift away. *Le Petit Parisien, L'Echo de Paris, Le Matin,* and *La Petite Gironde* all published articles on Mangin in May and June in which she was not even mentioned among the families continuing to claim him;[41] worse yet, *La Croix* reported that since the Monjoins had made their case, Lucie Lemay, along with the Vayssettes, the Brilles, the Rondots, the Dulongs, and the Mangins, had given up claims to Anthelme Mangin.[42] *L'Excelsior* and *Le Mémorial des Deux-Sèvres,* however, remained faithful to her, as did the newsletter of the Republican Association of Veterans, which took the opportunity to blast the government (as it was in the habit of doing):

> For three years now, the minister of pensions has been in possession of all the evidence we have published in the past few days and has responded by stonewalling. . . . Is a serious investigation really being conducted in good faith by the ministry? Certainly not. In addition to the minister's silence, there is the ill will of the National Veterans Union and the

League for the Rights of Man, who have also been entangled in this miserable affair. We are almost tempted to write that the minister does not want to examine the troubling matter submitted to him. Does the state have a special interest in seeing the unknown veteran under the Arc de Triomphe matched by the unknown veteran of Rodez?[43]

At least the Republican Association of Veterans was in accord with other veterans' organizations in demanding that Mangin be treated as something better than a lunatic, since he was both a hero and a victim: "Let us ask first that Mangin-Lemay be hospitalized elsewhere than in a madhouse. We owe homage to this comrade from the battlefields, whose vast butchery of 1914 turns the memory upside down."[44] Regarding one opinion as insufficient, the Republican Association of Veterans adopted the same point of view as *La Croix,* which on May 30, 1931, demanded more dignified treatment for the Rodez amnesiac, "this poor little French soldier, a victim like so many of his brothers in arms,"[45] and suggested moving him to a charitable institution. The *Journal des mutilés et combattants* went further, tying Anthelme Mangin's destiny to that of the four thousand other insane veterans of war in French asylums at the beginning of the thirties: "They must not be considered human refuse but victims of duty, and for this reason must be accorded the utmost comfort and consideration."[46] But nothing changed. Anthelme Mangin remained in Rodez, and preparation of the case for trial was exceedingly lengthy. It was not until May 8, 1933, that the state prosecutor in Aveyron, prior to ruling on the procedure that would be adopted to grant Mangin his identity, decided to conduct a final, and completely useless, experiment.

The idea was to put the amnesiac back in his familial surroundings—to take him back to his childhood haunts and observe his reactions. The Ministry of Pensions, not wishing to cross the Ministry of Justice, authorized Mangin's transfer to Châteauroux but did not conceal its doubts about an experiment it considered certain to fail. Citing the diagnosis that Professor Albert Claude of the Paris medical school had reached, Pensions pointed out that Mangin was not a simple amnesiac, "and that to force him to talk would only reinforce his negativistic tendencies."[47] The Aveyron prefect contacted his colleague in the Indre department and it was decided that, given Mangin's docile state, he would be placed in the Châteauroux hospital instead of a madhouse, the nearest of which was in Limoges. The transfer took place on September 15, 1933.

No record of this experiment is preserved in the Rodez archives. However, the press covered Mangin's transfer and his return to Saint-Maur-sur-Indre. *Le Progrès de l'Indre,* for example, closely followed the effort to shock the unknown man into recognition. Beginning on March 11, 1933, the newspaper came out strongly in favor of Mangin's transfer: "If this man is really the Monjoin son, maybe, on seeing the places where he spent his childhood, a glimmer of intelligence will pass through his brain and prompt a movement or a gesture showing that he recognizes the place he lived."[48] The operation took place on September 27, 1934. An automobile dropped Mangin off at the Saint-Maur train station, leaving him free to go where he wanted. Without hesitation, even though the road forked and the town lay hidden behind a row of poplars, the amnesiac, his mustache shaved as in earlier times, set out toward the village.[49] As he passed by, people looked at him, silently for the most part, and a few confirmed that he was Octave Monjoin. His first stop was the Café Carmillot, where he sat down a while before resuming his way toward rue du Moulin, where his father's and grandfather's houses stood.[50] With the same decisiveness, he entered his father's house but, recognizing Pierre Monjoin no more than he had his brother, remained detached, displaying no emotion. The representatives of the court observing the operation suggested to Mangin that he go to the school he had attended in his youth, and the amnesiac went.[51] When he returned to the car and was driven by the church, he uttered his only words of the day: "The church has changed." In fact, lightning had destroyed the bell tower some years earlier, and the restoration was clearly visible, as the article in *Match* pointed out.[52]

The experiment appeared to be conclusive—except for the protests registered by the other families, who denounced it as a masquerade and demanded that the operation be repeated in their own cities and villages. *La Dépêche,* which had taken Marthe Mazat's side, was incensed: "What an odious comedy, not to say sacrilege, is being played out around this pitiful victim of the war. . . ."[53] To *Le Matin,* which came down in favor of the Monjoins, Lucie Lemay dispatched a vehement telegram: "Mme. Lemay, mother of three children, a resident of Coulonges (Deux-Sèvres department), who has always claimed the Rodez amnesiac as her husband, protests against the affirmations that the unknown man called Anthelme Mangin has recognized Saint-Maur-sur-Indre as the place where he lived before the war."[54] She challenged the experiment as "predetermined": Mangin had been surrounded and followed and could have been unconsciously guided to the Monjoins' house, where he had recognized nothing.[55] *She,* on the other hand, as she insisted, had been recognized. Having learned from the press that Mangin was in Châteauroux, she went to the hospital there, and in front of the police the unknown man once again kissed her, as he had on their first encounter in Rodez.[56] The *Journal des mutilés et combattants,* which published a somewhat skeptical article on October 8, 1933, titled "Has the Rodez Amnesiac Been Identified?" renounced all hope the following month: "The enigma remains intact, and while all these poor people bustle around him, the Rodez amnesiac hangs on to his secret. Let us hope that, for his happiness and the peace of the families, the mystery will be solved in the end."[57]

In assessing the outcome of the Saint-Maur experiment, the state prosecutors in Châteauroux and Rodez had to conclude that it did not provide the information they were hoping for. In light of Mangin's mental state, they returned to Fenayrou's long-standing principle that testimony about resemblances, no matter how abundant, did not constitute irrefutable proof. The trial to determine the identity of the unknown soldier that was about to begin would therefore rely solely on administrative records, rather than on the dozens of witnesses who, on every side, were ready to recognize Mangin as their own.

Chapter Seven

The Double Death
of Anthelme Mangin

The Rodez amnesiac's legal files are nowhere to be found.[1] However, the tragedy this void represents for the historian is relative, because essentially the file would only contain the administrative papers the experts used to determine Anthelme Mangin's identity—papers we already know about, if not in their entirety, then at least in their conclusions. At this trial, unlike the Bruneri-Canella trial in Italy, no witnesses were heard. The crowd of people claiming to recognize Mangin would have added nothing to the judicial process.

Although the Saint-Maur-sur-Indre experiment had lasted only a single day—September 27, 1933—Anthelme Mangin remained in the hospital at Châteauroux until February 14, 1934. The Indre departmental prefect, in accord with his counterpart in Aveyron, thought it made sense to keep the patient in Châteauroux while he awaited the trial that would confirm him as Octave Monjoin, thus avoiding another transfer and its concomitant costs.[2] On January 29, 1934, the director of the hospital-asylum at Indre offered assurances that he saw no reason not to keep the amnesiac, whose habitual calm had been interrupted by only one crisis since his arrival the preceding year. But on January 31 Mangin was nevertheless ordered back to Rodez by the state prosecutor, who had finally received instructions from the Ministry of Justice as to the complex procedures to follow in reestablishing the patient's identity. One requirement was that Mangin remain in Rodez so that the court not be accused of partiality. Another was the naming of an *ad litem* attorney to represent Mangin's interests and to arraign all the families who claimed the amnesiac as a son or husband. Adolphe Benoît received this assignment from the Rodez court on March 21, 1934, and he soon heard from Pierre Monjoin, who, given the state of his finances, needed legal aid. Benoît issued summonses to the nineteen families claiming Mangin. Ten did not answer—including Louise Vayssettes, who could not come up with the necessary funds—which put them out of the running. Others simply gave up, saying they no longer recognized Mangin as their missing relative. In the end, four families persevered: Lucie Lemay; the widow Mangin from Nantes; Marthe Mazat; and Jeanne Mangin, a Saint-Brieuc woman who turned up late in the game, believing she recognized her husband, Edouard Mangin, in the amnesiac.[3]

Before the trial opened, yet another experiment was performed on Mangin in an attempt to shed light on his past. In September 1934, Fenayrou had retired, taking comfort in the certainty that he had located Mangin's real family after twelve trying years of defamation, tests, and useless face-to-face meetings. His replacement was Andrée Deschamps, a young woman who had interned at the Sainte-Anne asylum and had recently placed successfully in the competitive examination for candidates wishing to become doctors-in-charge at institutions for the insane.[4] Deschamps decided, just before the families were to gather in court, to induce a fever in the amnesiac via an artificially created abscess, so that she could question him in a feverish state. This method, introduced at the beginning of the century by Professor A. Fochier of the Lyon Medical School, had become common medical practice around 1910 and was used on patients with illnesses as diverse as influenza, pneumonia, meningitis, and puerperal infections. It consisted of an injection of 1 to 2 cc of essence of terebenthine, leading to an inflammatory reaction—that is, an abscess, which, once lanced, would allow the illness to come out, much in the manner of the abandoned practice of bleeding.[5] With the work of Jacques Roubinovitch in the 1920s, the procedure of artificially inducing abscesses won over psychiatry as an efficient therapeutic method.[6] So in inoculating Anthelme Mangin's thigh with 2 cc of terebenthine on January 12, 1935, Andrée Deschamps was following a recently developed and relatively common medical practice. The next day, a fever of around 102 degrees appeared and persisted for several days. On January 15, Mangin was questioned in his feverish state, which had indeed diminished his negativism. Asked to write his first and last names, the place and date of his birth, and the names of his father and his mother, he did so, and what he wrote accorded with Octave Monjoin's particulars.[7] One more item was added to the Monjoins' case, and their attorney would make use of it.

The trial opened on January 30, 1935. Although ordinarily nobody paid much attention to Aveyron court hearings, and courthouse functionaries and even those whose cases were being argued often were absent, this time the halls were packed with a mixture of journalists and curiosity seekers. Judge Berliat presided. The state prosecutor summarized the Rodez amnesiac's history, and then the various attorneys successively took the floor. Jean Marre, representing the Monjoins, presented his clients' evidence, emphasizing the information that the experiment at Saint-Maur and the artificially induced abscess had provided. Thereafter the attorneys Bauguil, Feyt, Bastide, Caldier, and David took their turns,[8] and a proceeding that should have been a formality, rapidly establishing the Monjoins' claim, turned against them instead. The astute arguments of Raoul David, of the Niort bar, representing Lucie Lemay, raised doubts in the judges' minds. In fact, all the Monjoins' arguments were disparaged and undermined, from Mangin's "predetermined" trip through the streets of Saint-Maur-sur-Indre to the artificially induced abscess, which, it was argued, proved nothing, since Mangin had heard the Monjoins spoken of so often.[9]

La Petite Gironde supported Lucie Lemay, recounting in a February 4 article David's "brilliant arguments, which strongly impressed the court," giving weight to the similarities between Mangin and Marcel Lemay, and casting doubt on Octave Monjoin: Sergeant Lemay's physical description matched the amnesiac's. He knew English, which he had learned at the Collège Chaptal in Paris. His former employer had averred that Mangin faultlessly wrote most of the names of mineral water he had dictated. In Châteauroux in 1933, Mangin had kissed the woman who believed herself to be his wife. And a former comrade from the Senne camp remembered having encountered Lemay leaning on a crutch after having broken his right leg. Then the photograph from Lucie Lemay's file had somehow disappeared, and the paper made ironic comparisons with the Stavisky affair, the financial and political scandal that was still shaking France. But David's secret weapon turned out to be Marcel Lemay's family history. His father had been interned in a mental institution for firing a revolver in the Place Clichy, and, according to his sister, Lemay bore a scar like Mangin's on his left wrist, because his mother had cut it when he was born, in the Beaujon Hospital in Paris, so that she could be sure to recognize him in case, as she feared, the infants were mixed up by accident. So doubt won out over the Monjoins' proof, and the Lemay camp triumphed, as *La Petite Gironde* reported:

> "These debates have cast light onto an affair that until now had been clouded by an administration convinced that the amnesiac could only be . . . Octave Monjoin. Now, after the illuminating speeches of M. David, it is no longer possible to believe this. Mme. Lemay's disturbing revelations, her irrefutable objections regarding the unknown man's identity, make some of the claims by the former director of the Rodez asylum completely unacceptable while at the same time

providing, beyond any doubt, sufficient proof to establish the identity of Marcel Lemay as the husband of the tobacconist of Coulonges."[10]

It was a case that should have been decided, after a brief deliberation, in a single day. Instead, to the despair of the Monjoins, Public Prosecutor Mittre decreed that the court could make no decision without a final evaluation by three *new* doctors and psychiatrists given complete powers to examine Mangin, including the liberty to repeat the experiment placing him in his ostensible family environment. The judges privately considered the matter while they waited for the results. Against all expectations, Lucie Lemay had won the first round.

The press reports on the progress of the trial presented the prosecutor's conclusions only partially. They included the naming of the three new experts, but their interpretations of the new experimental journey Mangin was to be sent on were twisted and wrong. Most of the papers reported that the Rodez amnesiac was going to be successively placed with the three families that claimed him.[11] This "rotating placement," each family getting three months, was mentioned in *Le Matin*,[12] *Le Journal des mutilés*,[13] *La Voix du combattant*,[14] *La Dépêche*,[15] and other papers. The source of the mistake was probably the article in *Le Matin*, which was reproduced by the newspapers that had not sent correspondents to Rodez. In any case, on the same day the minister of pensions became aware of the error, as well as of the artificially induced abscess that had been inflicted on the amnesiac, he wrote angrily to the attorney general. Outraged about Deschamps's procedure,

a "clearly excessive means of investigation," and about the rotating placement, he demanded that the dignity of the patient
be respected:

> If the information is true, then clearly we should be relieved
> that they did not have the idea of giving him successively to
> each of the thirteen families claiming him. But it is still true
> that during nine months this unfortunate lunatic must
> change his residence, his surroundings, and his habits three
> times; that three times he must submit to the fury of families
> trying to awaken his memories, and perhaps to their impa-
> tience following on the probable emptiness of their ef-
> forts. . . . I do not think anyone has the right to inflict such
> an ordeal on a patient whose state is precarious, whose men-
> tal condition is unbalanced, and who needs above all a calm
> and regular existence. . . .
>
> Whatever is in Mangin's interest, both physical and men-
> tal, must define the limits of the experiments permitted.[16]

The minister concluded by asking that the attorney general
apply pressure on the departmental prosecutor to oppose all
new experiments. The Ministry of Justice forwarded the letter to the Ministry of Health, which forwarded it to the Aveyron prefect; he received it on May 24 and forwarded it to the
prosecutor, who totally denied that there had been any plan
for a rotating placement. But he defended the artificially induced abscess, "which was not painful [and] presented no
danger. . . . Its use, which in this case yielded appreciable results, does not appear to me to have gone beyond the limits of

reasonable and humane treatment."[17] On the following June 17, Deschamps, informed by the departmental prosecutor of the minister of pensions' objections, also answered the accusations. Describing the artificially induced abscess as a commonplace, widely used treatment, she objected vehemently to the "aspersion cast on [her] professional dignity, and on the freedom of action that doctors maintain within the regulations. . . . I cannot accept this intrusion into a strictly medical domain," she continued, "which risks hindering the most legitimate and officially sanctioned of our therapeutic efforts in current medical practice."[18] Nevertheless, this vestige of a medical system that had once thought illness could be physically drawn from the body would disappear soon enough in the coming years.

Meanwhile, the decree the Rodez judgment issued on the evening of January 30 was carried out on March 6, when the three experts were named: a M. Paul, a Parisian doctor and jurist; Victor Truelle, the doctor in charge of the Sainte-Anne asylum in Paris; and Georges Génil-Perrin, the doctor in charge of asylums for the department of Seine. They had carte blanche to inspect the Mangin files, "to contact all specialists, to request any new investigations they did not feel they should conduct themselves (handwriting comparisons, etc.); to consider all evidence, to hear witnesses, to offer their opinion on the value of the information written down by Mangin on January 15, 1935; to proceed with any other measures they might judge useful, specifically all face-to-face meetings and trips involving Mangin; and, finally, to decide whether, based on their investigations, any certainty emerges that Mangin is the individual claimed by one of the families involved in the trial."[19] As soon as the experts were sworn in, Anthelme Mangin was to be sent to the Sainte-Anne asylum, where all the evaluations would take place.[20]

Thus, in an excess of scruple and zeal, the 1935 trial aborted, opening the way to yet another examination of Mangin's case—that is, a return to the point of departure. Once again, his identification was delayed until a hypothetical later date, always delayed. The failure of the court in this case went far beyond simple dithering, which might at least have been understandable. The court undermined its own responsibility by granting the privilege and the power of identifying Mangin to three leading medical experts whose conclusions it would simply rubber-stamp.

More than a year went by between the naming of experts, on March 6, 1935, and their swearing in before the Paris court, on March 27, 1936—an insignificant stretch for Mangin, but an eternity for the families who wanted him. They had to wait until March 11, 1936, for the minister of pensions to decide to transfer Mangin to a Seine asylum in accordance with the wishes of the police prefecture's department for the insane. On March 20, accompanied by a doctor and a caretaker, Anthelme Mangin left Rodez for good, bound for the region of Paris.[21] The next day he arrived at the Sainte-Anne asylum; from there he was finally sent to the Perray-Vaucluse Hospital, near Epinay-sur-Orge, on April 3.[22] And then everyone had to wait another year for the three experts to render their final verdict.

During this period, and particularly around the beginning of 1937, when the evaluation by the three doctors was beginning,

Mangin had become a celebrity. His face appeared in the Pathé newsreels that were projected on the screens of cinemas all over France. Occasionally, families who thought they recognized the amnesiac and who did not know about his transfer to Paris turned up at the Rodez asylum or the Aveyron prefecture—to little good, since the Ministry of Pensions was now refusing to complicate the procedure with new requests. In any case, the experts had decided to isolate Mangin in order to remove him from external influences that might disturb their work, and so no further permissions to visit him were being granted.[23] This decision created a drama for those who, thinking they recognized the amnesiac as a missing relative, sought some confirmation—such as Pierre Givet, who wrote the director of the Sainte-Anne asylum several times without receiving a reply. On September 29, 1936, he wrote the senator from the Loire department, Jean Taurines, requesting him to intervene on his behalf and see that he received a reply, positive or negative—because uncertainty was the worst torture.[24] On March 19, 1936, the day before Mangin's departure for Paris, *La Petite Gironde* reported that a large number of the inhabitants of Champagneux, in the department of Savoie, had recognized the unknown man as Louis Monnet, a resident of the city who had gone missing in Argonne in 1915.[25] The following year—to cite only one more example—the widow of Pierre Bounaix, from Allassac, in the department of Corrèze, gone missing in the Somme in 1916, claimed Mangin. Like Pierre Givet, she was refused permission to meet the amnesiac in Sainte-Anne; but her daughter and her son-in-law, wielding a recommendation from Charles Spinasse, the minister of the economy, were able to meet with the director of the asylum and give him records, which, however, did not help in identifying Mangin.[26]

Meanwhile, the families in the trial tried to take advantage of the experts' slowness as an opportunity to find new arguments to tip the balance in their favor—or, failing that, to convince some journalist who might faithfully relay their version of the facts. Lucie Lemay benefited from the support of Emmanuel Car in *L'Excelsior* and Yves Gaël in *Le Journal*. In February 1936, the latter published a long article all about Marcel Lemay with the portentous title "The Man Who Found His Name." Demanding that Mangin be sent to Vincennes so that he might recognize the place he had lived before leaving for the war, the newspaper looked ahead to the resolution of the enigma: "Let Mme. Lemay be reassured. Her husband will most likely be returned to her soon. His file is much too rich in all sorts of proof for his case to be dropped."[27]

Finally, on January 12, the experts called together the various families claiming to recognize Mangin, including those who had not surfaced before the Rodez trial in January 1935.[28] This group meeting, led by Génil-Perrin, took place in the Henri-Rousselle Hospital, in the presence of Anthelme Mangin, who, to shield himself from all the families who were looking at him or calling out to him, sometimes hid his face in his hands, sometimes behind the hat of his uniform.[29] Hauled up onto a platform for a search for distinguishing traits cited by this person or that, he was forced to undress in spite of his modesty; he tried to hide behind a blackboard but eventually followed the doctor's order docilely.[30] The specialists could very well have dispensed with this last test, having confirmed in the preceding days the "negativistic ironic" aspect of Mangin's affliction—that is, his propensity to impede his identification and "to make fun of those who were anxiously hovering over him."[31] *Le Matin* called him a faker, a demented man who may have lost his reason but who on several occasions had been caught "red-handed in untruths."[32] For that reason, the presence or absence of the traits indicated by the families had to be publicly determined.

Among those present at the meeting were Lucie Lemay, assisted by her two attorneys, René Russier, of the Paris bar, and Raoul David, of the Niort bar; Marthe Mazat; and Anselme Patureau-Mirand, the upstanding mayor of Saint-Maur-sur-Indre, who had once again donned his lawyer's robe to represent the Monjoins, who were unable to make the trip. The widow Mangin, on the other hand, refused to participate, denouncing the meeting as a charade intended to award her son to another family. In the press, in particular *L'Oeuvre, L'Intransigeant,* and *La Petite Gironde,* she waxed indignant:

> He is my son! They have to give him back to me. . . .
>
> I formally oppose the idea that my son, Roger, whom my sister and I found "prisoner" in an insane asylum in Rodez, be given to another family. I am convinced that, in the familiar surroundings of his childhood, Roger would recover his lucidity. . . .
>
> I am formally refusing to participate in an evaluation without witnesses who knew my son in his regiment, having painful memories of the Rodez evaluation in May 1923, when everything had been prepared counter to the truth.[33]

The meeting was not public; only the claimant families were allowed to attend. Journalists were barred, so they were left to find out what had happened from the families, who of course tended to present their own version of the facts in the light most favorable to them. Buoyed by her first victory, in January 1935, Lucie Lemay said she felt confident. In an interview with Emmanuel Car of *L'Excelsior* the day before the meeting, she declared, "I always felt confident. At the beginning of the trial I was alone with my advisers in the presence of a hundred families. But I knew that it would be acknowledged that I was right, not only because I am the only person the patient has recognized, but also because I can present absolutely incontestable anatomical arguments. I will be present tomorrow for the meeting of the experts, and I dare to hope that my husband will soon be returned to me."[34] Twenty years after the end of the Great War, the daily concluded, Anthelme Mangin, the "living unknown soldier," was going to find his family: "We will not hide the fact that Mme. Lemay's chances are great."[35] While this evaluation would indeed prove decisive, it was not Lucie Lemay who would again create the surprise, but the Monjoins' attorney, who produced an unexpected piece of evidence that established Mangin's identity definitively.

When Patureau-Mirand's turn to plead before the experts arrived, he went over the various strong points of the Monjoins' case before coming to the new item that the press was to describe as "earthshaking." It was a letter of April 6, 1936, from the director of the asylum at Bron to Edouard Herriot, the mayor of Lyon—who had forwarded it to the Ministry of

Pensions—affirming that, in fact, Mangin had never been lost.[36] The story of the discovery of the amnesic soldier wandering the platforms of the Lyon-Brotteaux railway station had been pure invention. On the contrary, Anthelme Mangin had been part of a convoy of repatriated invalids sent directly to Bron from the German hospital at Königsberg on January 31, 1918. On his arrival, on February 1, the unknown man was of course unable to say his name, and he was given the name Anthelme Mangin based on the best interpretation of his babbling. Research carried out in the German archives in 1931 by the Ministry of Pensions revealed that on January 31, 1918, Octave Monjoin had been in the hospital at Königsberg, ill with dementia praecox and awaiting repatriation.[37]

Hence there could be no further doubt, and *L'Excelsior,* which had previously lined up behind Lucie Lemay, completely changed its tune and declared that proof of Mangin's identity was now certain: "Anthelme Mangin was Octave Monjoin!"[38] *La Petite Gironde,* which had also unconditionally supported Mme. Lemay, now regarded the Monjoins' case with increased interest but expressed outrage that a piece of evidence as important as the one unveiled by M. Patureau-Mirand could have remained unknown until 1937: "Wasn't it strange that a document that could have liberated a glorious soldier of the Great War from the tawdry insane asylum where he was locked up for eighteen years took so long to emerge from the administration's files?"[39] For her part, Lucie Lemay refused to capitulate and decided, with the aid of her lawyers, to likewise follow her husband's trail, starting from the German archives. Still, there was hardly any doubt about the verdict the three experts would render. On March 11, the report arrived at the Rodez court and was made public: as expected, the doctors Paul, Truelle, and Génil-Perrin recognized Anthelme Mangin as Octave Monjoin.[40] The magistrates maintained their freedom to make the final decision, but it was now clear that the judgment could no longer go against the Monjoins.

So the Monjoins were impatient. "There is, in Saint-Maur, an eighty-four-year-old man who would like to kiss the son he has not seen since 1914. . . . Let him not wait too much longer," *Le Département* and *Le Progrès de l'Indre* both declared in January 1937.[41] On April 10, one month after the experts' verdict, the two Indre newspapers protested the slowness in rendering justice and described the situation as drama turned into vaudeville. In fact, that month, another mother, Mme. Thiesen, a Parisian street merchant, had recognized her son in the amnesiac and hired a renowned lawyer, J.-C. Legrand, to argue for her. These developments slowed things down, and what with proceeding from one dismissal to another, "Mangin would be dead before finding his name and his family," the papers fumed. "There are cases in which justice should not wait; there are a few—like the one at hand—in which there is a duty to move rapidly, especially after so many lost years."[42] On May 29, *Le Progrès de l'Indre* launched a new attack against the procrastinations of the Rodez court, pointing to the Monjoins' sorrow; to the financial difficulties of Octave's aged father, who was being deprived of a pension; and also to the murky and underhanded arguments of the other families persisting in claiming a man who, to all appearances, was not their relative:

The effect of such a delay is depressing. An eighty-four-year-old man goes on living without the slightest help from the state.

Can the Rodez court . . . end the long ordeal of a family that, unlike the others, never sought any financial advantage by requesting the identification of their son? . . .

Can those who have acted otherwise reflect and understand that their efforts are bound to fail? They may have been in good faith earlier; but protesting the conclusions of the experts' report is proof that affection is not a sufficient explanation for their behavior.[43]

Thus, the old theory of families' greed for Mangin's "fortune"—the pension he had accumulated since his reclassification as a lunatic—raised its head in the case of the Monjoins. Even today, among the witnesses interviewed in Saint-Maur and the descendants of the families involved, accusations of venality keep popping up on all sides to explain the fury and tenacity of the various families. It is true that in the Monjoins' case, the financial question *was* important: Pierre Monjoin's claim for the pension due the parent of a soldier who had died for France was what had resurrected the attempt to identify Mangin in 1930. The discovery of the amnesiac son and his accumulated indemnity was a windfall for this family of modest peasants, who would benefit from both those funds and the continuing pension, and they could request a parental pension as legitimately for a man driven insane by the war as for a soldier killed on the battlefield.[44] Unlike Lucie Lemay, who dreamed only of caring for the lunatic in whom she saw her traumatized husband, the Monjoin family did not seek guardianship of Mangin. They simply expressed the wish, apart from their interest in his pension, that the patient be interned in the closest asylum—that is, in Limoges, more than eighty kilometers from Saint-Maur, or, preferably, in the asylum for the incurable at Châteauroux.[45] Nothing would change for Anthelme Mangin, an eternal lodger in mental institutions; he would get his name back but not his old surroundings or the affection and care of a family. But justice, in this case, had to be rendered not on the basis of family love but on the basis of records and facts, without regard for what might become of Mangin.

In truth, none of the families the Monjoins suspected of wanting Mangin's money were motivated by greed. They were all convinced that the amnesiac was their dear missing child or husband, the one over whom they had shed so many tears, whom they had never been able to forget and who had now, by some incredible miracle, returned to them. Génil-Perrin understood this situation well, and he predicted that his report would do nothing to alter the rejected families' determination: "Will a decision of the court suffice to change the heart of an old mama clinging for ten years now to this final hope?"[46] *L'Ancien Combattant de Paris* agreed, observing "that this lamentable and painful affair, which for twenty years now has dragged the evaluations of experts and the experts themselves into court, has finally ended, and may it not reawaken as long as anyone involved remains alive."[47] That wish would be thoroughly denied, and the fears behind it borne out beyond what anyone could imagine.

On October 12, 1937, the trial that was intended to establish Anthelme Mangin's identity once and for all began. The experts' decision in favor of the Monjoins was being opposed by four families—the Saint-Brieuc Mangins, the Nantes Mangins, the Lemays, and the Mazats—who had united to demand a new investigation whose direction they would determine.

Marthe Mazat, who had no real proofs of identity and who wanted the verdict to rely on resemblance alone, demanded the dismissal of the administrative inquiry. She still hoped that the testimony of her son's former comrades would be admitted and that the report of the Ministry of Pensions, which she thought had been partial to the Monjoins since 1931, would be rejected. But her suspicions as to the integrity of the ministry were ill founded. Professor Sorel had rejected her case long before 1931; the experts named by the Rodez court in 1935 had simply renewed the objections he had formulated on June 10, 1923. None of the distinguishing marks indicated by Mme. Mazat and her lawyer, M. Caldier, of the Saint-Affrique bar, had been found on the amnesiac, not even those Mme. Mazat had cited at the evaluation in 1923 and verified in January 1937, at Sainte-Anne: a reddish spot on the left buttock and a scar on the penis. The list furnished by Mme. Mazat changed more than once in the course of the hearing, and her demand that Mangin be placed in his past environment, in Dordogne, was medically dubious, given that the amnesiac, as a negativist, could never recover his memory. Hence Marthe Mazat was soon out of the running.

The widow Mangin, née Le Pommelet, from Saint-Brieuc, was also quickly dispatched: her husband, it turned out, had never been taken prisoner. After he was demobilized, on February 13, 1919, he had simply dropped out of contact and had never reappeared in the conjugal home.

As for the widow Mangin from Nantes, the most pugnacious of the group, her case appeared quite hollow. She produced no records to support the theory that she had propounded. Like Mme. Mazat, she demanded that Mangin be brought to Nantes, to the putative site of his childhood, and confronted by his former friends, who would recognize him. The judges knew perfectly well that she had not prevailed in 1923, when, at her insistence, an expert had been named to decide among the nine families then claiming Mangin—her son was two inches taller than the lunatic. In addition, she refused to cooperate with the experts, whom she considered hostile, and did not even deign to attend the group meeting of January 12, 1937, at Sainte-Anne. She, too, was conclusively dismissed. The final showdown was really between Lucie Lemay and the Monjoins.

Like the others, Lucie Lemay gave little credence to the findings in the report by the three doctors, and she demanded a new investigation authorizing the transfer of Mangin to Vincennes. Further, she questioned the veracity of the irrefutable records produced by the German authorities, which aligned Mangin, interned in Bron on February 1, 1918, with the patient Octave Monjoin, repatriated on January 31. She demanded that the originals of documents stored mainly at the Ministry of

Pensions (there were also some at Foreign Affairs) be produced. This demand, predicated on her suspicion of partiality, surprised the judges, who stressed that the originals were required to remain in the archives and that the copies were "sufficiently guaranteed as to their truthfulness by the authorities who, with no prejudice regarding the case, had sent them."[48] While the descriptions of Marcel Lemay and the amnesiac matched, the distinguishing characteristics his wife had noted—for example, a deformed knee and a mole on the left groin—could not be found. Evaluations of handwriting and anthropometry (from a photograph furnished by Lucie Lemay) were also unfavorable. Mangin knew English, like Marcel Lemay, but, unlike him, neither Latin nor German. That he had correctly spelled a number of mineral waters proved nothing: Octave Monjoin would also have known them from his work as a waiter.

The Monjoins' case was then heard. Anselme Patureau-Mirand, the mayor of Saint-Maur, assisted by M. Marre of the Rodez bar, deftly laid out his clients' position. With Octave Monjoin, everything matched: description, handwriting, anthropometry. Although the Monjoin son had dropped out of contact in his second year of captivity, he had never in fact disappeared. His file, furnished by the German authorities, indicated a fracture to the right leg and his evolution into dementia praecox; it was owing to this latter condition that he was evacuated on January 31, 1918, along with sixty-five other madmen being repatriated from Germany, as part of a convoy that arrived in Bron the next day. Unable to speak his name clearly, he was registered under the name Anthelme Mangin—a version of his babbled response. Finally, the Saint-

Maur experiment of 1933 and the artificially induced abscess of January 1935 had both confirmed the Monjoins' theory, as had yet another 1937 interrogation by experts, who asked him the number of his regiment and heard him answer the 95th, the one in which Octave Félicien Monjoin had served. When the hearing ended and the case was sent out for deliberation, no one was betting on Lucie Lemay's chances any longer. On November 16, 1937, the Rodez court brought in its verdict: Anthelme Mangin was Octave Monjoin.[49]

The living unknown soldier, who had impassioned public opinion and even inspired a trip to Rodez by a Paramount Pictures team intent on making a movie (which never materialized), was no more: he had found his name. On November 16, at 5:30 P.M., M. Rascalou of the Rodez bar announced the good news by telegram to his colleague, Anselme Patureau-Mirand, who, accompanied by a journalist, went immediately to the Monjoins'. The neighbors came running, bottles of wine were opened, tears flowed, and everyone celebrated. The fight being over, *Le Progrès de l'Indre* could demand quick action from the Ministry of Pensions: "The old father Monjoin must now obtain his parental pension, and quickly."[50]

But it was not to be. The other families had not yet had their final say. *L'Ancien Combattant de Paris* launched an appeal for reason in its columns, discouraging the inevitable appeal and expressing the wish "that this doleful trial not start up again and that the Monjoin case remain conclusively decided."[51] *L'Union catholique,* the clerical newspaper of Aveyron, was more pessimistic: the vigorous defense presented by the families at the October 12 hearing "makes us imagine that the Montpellier court of appeals is likely to become the next scene of a drama that has long impassioned the country."[52]

The widow Mangin of Saint-Brieuc dropped out. The other families appealed. Marthe Mazat, Lucie Lemay, and the widow Mangin from Nantes were now joined by Mme. Thiesen, the Parisian who had come late to the case (in February 1937). The four of them pleaded their case on December 12 and 13, 1938, continuing on January 12, 1939, but presenting no new facts.[53] On March 8, 1939, the Montpellier court of appeals upheld the Rodez court's verdict.[54] With its outcome so utterly predictable, this last appeal had served no real purpose, but as long as it had lasted—more than a year—Mangin had not been awarded to the Monjoins, his identity had not been confirmed, and the four litigating families could still hope. Now hope was dashed, as Jacques Decaen of the *Journal des mutilés* well understood:

> This legal decision constitutes the last act in one of the most moving tragedies born of the war, a tragedy that saw families who yearned for their missing relative battle in good faith and with infinitely admirable stubbornness so that a poor wreck from the conflict might come take his place among them—a place that the Montpellier judges' verdict will, alas, leave forever empty in too many homes where the judgment has brutally extinguished a flame of hope that had burned for twenty-one years.[55]

In Saint-Maur, on the other hand, everyone rejoiced at this "humane and just decision. . . . The hour of justice strikes for the second time in favor of one of the war's greatest surviving victims."[56] Anselme Patureau-Mirand went to the Monjoins' modest home, as he had in November 1937, to announce the verdict, bringing with him several bottles of good wine, and he toasted the victory with a few simple words: "Finally, it's done!" But the family's joy was bittersweet. Pierre Monjoin was by now a very old man, in fragile health. His son Joseph was no better off, having been bedridden for months with chest pains caused by a kick from a horse so severe that he had required surgery. At least Joseph Monjoin, who knew that his days were numbered, could take some comfort in the fact that his brother had finally found his name: "Ah! I thought I would kick the bucket[57] before this decision came through," he cried from his bedroom. "The last years of my life were just for this. I'm so happy, very happy."[58] After the drinking, though, a final worry surfaced. Old Pierre Monjoin asked his mayor and attorney, "But is it really finished?"

His concern was well founded, because there was still one final recourse: the supreme court. And Lucie Lemay did appeal to this final venue. "The trial was thus far from being over," *Le Mémorial des Deux-Sèvres* noted gloomily.[59]

Pierre Monjoin never got his pension. He died on April 1, 1939, shortly after his son Joseph, who had succumbed to his injuries on March 23.[60] Less than a month after the Montpellier court of appeals had rendered its verdict, there were no more Monjoins to carry on the fight to identify Mangin. The protractedness of the judicial process and the successive appeals of the other families had kept deferring identification of the amnesiac until, finally, the plaintiffs had disappeared. From that point on, "the Rodez amnesiac was more alone than ever," as *Le Courrier de l'Aveyron*[61] lamented. Of course there was still Gisèle Monjoin, the daughter that Joseph, an early widower, had reared on his own and who had kept the family afloat on her salary alone. Born after the war, she had known her uncle only through her father's and grandfather's stories, and today she acknowledges that, in accord with her family's peasant background, emotions were seldom demonstratively or expansively expressed and there was little discussion of Mangin. "We worked and we didn't talk about that much," she remembered. Aside from the judicial struggle, no personal memory connects her to the amnesiac.

The illustrated magazine *Match* devoted its issue of April 13, 1939, to the final act of the tragedy, which was Anthelme Mangin's loss of his family before he had really found them: "The asylum door, half opened, closed on the amnesiac again. The soldier found his name but not his destiny."[62] In reality, Mangin had not found even his name yet, because the supreme court appeal had delayed the definitive judgment. So *Le Courrier de l'Aveyron* was right in observing that "the drama of the Rodez amnesiac had not yet reached its epilogue."[63] As it turned out, Mangin never found his identity at all. The supreme court's work on his case was interrupted by the war, before it was halted—this time for good—by Anthelme Mangin's death, on September 10, 1942. No pension file in the name of Octave Monjoin was opened in the archives, and Gisèle Monjoin reports that she never inherited anything from her uncle—proof that justice was never done. Anthelme Mangin, even though he was twice identified as Octave Monjoin—first by the Rodez court, and then by the Montpellier court of appeals—was not officially, formally recognized.

His end was pitiful. After the evaluation at Sainte-Anne in January 1937, he was returned to the Vaucluse asylum and spent monotonous days there, no longer punctuated, as they had been at Rodez, by visits from Louise Vayssettes and Marthe Mazat. During the ensuing war and the occupation, he was certainly affected by the food rationing that led to the starvation of between 40,000 and 50,000 patients in insane asylums (which had become psychiatric hospitals by decree in 1938). That drama, long hidden from historians,[64] was not simply a voluntary choice to eliminate those "without value," following the eugenic model of Nazi Germany; rather, it followed from the administration's inertia, which condemned residents of psychiatric hospitals to underfeeding at the same time that civil hospitals were getting supplementary rations. Although the decline in French population had effectively prevented the French from lining up behind German programs to sterilize and exterminate the mentally ill,[65] eugenics propagandists had nonetheless prepared the way for indifference toward the desperate situation of psychiatric hospitals between 1940 and 1944. Daily life in the asylums during the Second World War was horrific: patients fought with each other for larger portions; the strong stole rations from the weak; starving inmates picked through garbage cans and were even known to eat the bark of trees or their own excrement.[66] Mangin, with his dementia praecox, would have suffered particularly in this struggle for survival, because in his detachment he was in no condition to protect his meager rations. In 1931 Jean Aicardi, the correspondent for *Le Petit Marseillais,* had already noted that the amnesiac ate normally but only with help: "If no one invited him to do so, he would never eat, because he shows no desire to feed himself."[67] Weakened by undereating, Anthelme Mangin died on September 10, 1942, at 7:30 A.M., in the Sainte-Anne hospital, to which he had been transferred on August 28 for an operation on his right leg, where his wound had reopened. The death certificate was made out in the name of Octave Monjoin, the administration having adopted the Rodez and Montpellier court decisions posthumously.[68]

Completely forgotten since the outbreak of war in 1939, Anthelme Mangin was buried in a common grave in the Bagneux cemetery. The story of the living unknown soldier would have ended there if Emmanuel Car, who had followed the case attentively for *L'Excelsior,* had not devoted a final article to the tragic conclusion of his life. The opening of the film *The Traveler without Luggage,* in 1944, provided the journalist with an occasion to return to the "great enigma that provoked the world for more than twenty years" but that was now forgotten. In the columns of the Marseille weekly *Actu,* he recounted the whole story fairly faithfully, including the last days of the man who now lay in an obscure common grave in the suburbs of Paris, "without a cross, without flowers, without even a corner of anonymous earth."[69] When Marcel Boucton, a timber broker in Reims, read this article, he became incensed that this First World War soldier, long a symbol of grief and suffering, had been so scorned and abused in death. He resolved to restore Mangin's dignity, writing on March 28, 1944, to the mayor of Saint-Maur-sur-Indre:

Monsieur Mayor,

According to a story in the newspaper *Actu*, dated March 12, 1944, and written by Emmanuel Car, a final judgment on March 8, 1939, definitively identified the unfortunate Octave Monjoin as the son of M. Pierre Monjoin, your deceased constituent.

According to this same story, Octave Monjoin lies in an anonymous tomb in the Bagneux cemetery.

Moved by this article, I immediately went to investigate the site, and I had a monument placed at his tomb, with a cross bearing the necessary inscriptions.

But I believe that Octave Monjoin deserves much better. I am writing with an offer to see to his reinterment in your local cemetery, and I agree to cover *all expenses* for this reinterment, because I would like for him to be able to lie with his own people, who claimed him steadfastly but in vain, missing the joy of seeing their claim satisfied while they were alive.

In case this is impossible, I will make all the necessary arrangements to keep his tomb from suffering the unacceptable lot of common graves.

This soldier, without an identity for twenty years of his life, must not be abandoned like an old wreck—quite the contrary![70]

The Saint-Maur municipal council agreed to Boucton's proposal, granting the amnesiac a permanent grave in the area reserved for those who "died for France," and decreeing that his body lie alone there.[71] Yet between Marcel Boucton's request and the actual return of Mangin's body, several more years would pass.

For her part, Lucie Lemay had not given up. For a while the departure of her son, Louis, for war distracted her from her anguish; she lived in fear of losing him as she had lost her husband twenty-five years earlier. He was taken prisoner and returned home in 1943. By then Lucie Lemay was exhausted from a lifetime of struggle; her iron will had given way to a general fragility. She was aware that Anthelme Mangin had died in the Sainte-Anne asylum and that, with his death, the court had closed his case; but she asked her son to contact her attorney and find out whether there was a procedure for continuing the struggle and securing a postmortem identification. Louis Lemay, who had been suffering the consequences of his mother's obsession since 1927—other children had humiliated him by calling him the madman's son—had no interest in pursuing the affair. The second generation did not take up the torch, hoping instead to forget the Great War and its effects. Anthelme Mangin was dead? So much the better. When Lucie Lemay died, in 1954, Louis promptly burned the thick file she had put together, including all the newspaper articles about her, thus symbolically ending his mother's ordeal, which had also been his own.[72] But Lucie Lemay's granddaughter has revived her crusade. In 2003, she requested that Mangin's body be exhumed and a DNA test be performed to establish his identity.

In 1948, Anthelme Mangin was exhumed from his common grave and buried in the Saint-Maur-sur-Indre cemetery, in a ceremony still alive in the memories of the oldest villagers. On March 23, 1948, shortly before the body was to arrive, the daily *Centre-Éclair* retraced the Rodez amnesiac's history and his relatives' legal battle. On April 1 the paper published the program for Octave Monjoin's funeral, which was to last from Friday, April 2, to Sunday, April 4. The entire town was invited to the chapel and to the funeral, "to bear witness to the sorrowful existence of our compatriot and to share the sympathy we feel for his family and, in particular, his niece." The ceremony consisted of several stages, which made those three days in April 1948 into a kind of Armistice Day reincarnated as a patriotic Easter, with the lowering into his grave of a soldier once unknown but now reclaimed under gilded veterans' flags. There were four principal parts: the presentation of the casket in the city hall on Friday and Saturday; the paying of respects and the gathering of veterans; the funeral mass, on Sunday morning; and the afternoon procession to the final burial.[73]

Mangin's body arrived on Friday morning at precisely six o'clock. The mayor, M. Bourdier, and the president of the veterans' association received the body at the Saint-Maur railway station. From there it was carried to city hall, which had been transformed for the occasion into a chapel. The walls of the main hall were draped with vast curtains on which were hung flags—of veterans, of firemen, of the Saint Vincent Society, of the Saint-Maur Sports Union, and of those inducted in 1911, a group that included Octave Monjoin. The first ceremony took place in the presence of his remaining family members: his niece, Gisèle Monjoin (now Boulbon by marriage), an aunt, and an uncle. The priest, Father Trinquard, blessed the casket, and then for two days the people of Saint-Maur passed by Monjoin's remains, flanked day and night by veterans from 1914–1918 and 1939–1945. The next day, at 3:00 P.M., the Reims delegation arrived in Châteauroux. Headed by Marcel Boucton, it included twenty-one members— heads of veterans' associations, both local and departmental; priest-veterans, Second World War prisoners, deportees or insubordinates forced by the Service du Travail Obligatoire to work in Germany. There was a little boy in the delegation named Jean Pottelain, the son of a Resistance fighter shot by the Nazis. Everyone in France who had fought in the two wars was represented, and memories of the two conflicts were thus enshrined in a single national cult.

After a brief reception organized by Anselme Patureau-Mirand, the erstwhile mayor of Saint-Maur who had worked so hard to win the Monjoins' case, the cortège proceeded toward city hall, where the veterans from Reims met their brothers from Indre and gathered before the casket. On Sunday morning, the whole village gathered for the ceremony; the church was too small to contain the crowd. Not until 3:30 P.M. was the body taken from the chapel, joining a procession led by firemen, the disabled, veterans, partisans of the Resistance, former prisoners, and those who had been forced to labor abroad. Monjoin's family came next; then the town's elected representatives; and, finally, at the head of the citizens of Saint-Maur, the schoolchildren, led by their teachers. The veterans dominated a ceremony they had organized and which they naturally directed. They were the pallbearers, they flanked the body, they occupied places of honor at the church and in the cortège in front of the few remaining members of Monjoin's family, in a demonstration that the Rodez amnesiac's interment was not a private burial for Monjoin the lunatic but, rather, a collective ceremony honoring the unknown living soldier, martyr of the Great War, around whom both the community and France had drawn together in suffering. At only one moment did Monjoin's relatives take the principal role: after the burial, after three speeches and a final prayer, and after several shovelfuls of soil had been spread on the casket, the crowd slowly filed out of the Saint-Maur cemetery, offering their condolences to the family. Monjoin's remains, in the earth where they belonged at last, had found their identity, their pitiful identity as a lost soul from the Great War. The living unknown soldier had been honored as he deserved.

Conclusion

On April 4, 1948, at the tomb of Anthelme Mangin—once again Octave Félicien Monjoin—the mayor of Saint-Maur pronounced a final word before the casket was lowered into the earth:

> His remains have returned to us. He will be better off with his own family in his final resting place. He has come home.
>
> May this soil of Berry, his native land, in which he will lie, rest light upon him.
>
> We soon forget those who are no more. But your presence in our cemetery, Félicien, will perpetuate for us the memory of the lamentable trail that for twenty-five years made a living dead man of you.[1]

Nevertheless, Mangin *was* forgotten. The tragic destiny of the living unknown soldier was erased from the memory of all but a few old Saint-Maur locals and the few people close to the story. Only the regional press shared any interest in Mangin's reburial. The French lost interest in his case after the Montpellier Court of Appeals handed down its verdict, and perhaps even earlier—when the Rodez court issued its first verdict in November 1937. Justice having been done, the allure faded from the mystery surrounding the Rodez amnesiac, and the newspapers could not be bothered with a case that no longer held suspense.

But this prosaic explanation is not quite sufficient. It ignores the questions of memory and oblivion, censorship, amnesia and hypermnesia—all of which are charged with meaning. The living unknown soldier had been a concrete symbol of grief and suffering whose story was recounted again and again in the press until 1939. While his celebrity seemed natural—inevitable in a nation in mourning, when death lurked everywhere—the indifference that quickly engulfed him seems incomprehensible. One explanation, perhaps, may be found in Giraudoux's *Siegfried*, where the amnesiac hero draws his strength and power from his affliction: "His amnesia gave your Siegfried a past, nobility. . . . If he should find his family or his memory, he will become our equal."[2] Indeed, the moment Anthelme Mangin was identified, his iconic status as the living dead who stood for all those who were gone had vanished. By acquiring a name, a past, a family, he returned to the world of the living. The journalist Jean Aicardi grasped this in 1931, when the Monjoins first made their appearance; he wrote that the Rodez amnesiac "is no longer the unknown living soldier. He is a miserable wreck from the war who's going to have a name."[3] A "wreck," a "poor vet,"[4] a "madman,"[5] a "poor nut"[6] —that is what Mangin became when he lost the thing that had made him exceptional: his lack of a name and of a past. After the decision of the court of appeals, the Rodez amnesiac attained the same anonymity as all the other lunatics locked up in French asylums. Although nothing changed for him, the anguish he had caused his contemporaries—the disorder provoked by this symbol of the missing from the Great War—was at an end. Mangin had returned to nothingness.

And finally the Second World War closed the case by ending the mourning begun in 1918, tossing the myth of Colonel Chabert—born of the guilt of the living toward the dead—onto the ash heap of anxieties. The First World War had left France morally defeated, without resources or energy, with a sense of accelerated decadence and Pyrrhic victory. The 1944 liberation, however, inaugurated a new, reformed France, revitalized by Resistance ideals and an energized population. The references had changed: the hero of 1918 was the dead veteran, mourned in endless ceremonies, while the hero of 1944 was the living Resistance fighter who had triumphed over barbarism. With confidence in the future, with dignity and liberty regained, guilt vanished. The theme of the return of the missing had lost its shock value. Instead, with *La Cuisine au beurre* (*Cooking with Butter*), by Gilles Grangier (1963)—in which André, the second husband, is faced with the delayed return from Germany of Fernand, the officially dead first husband—it had turned into comedy.

But if the Second World War was far less damaging to France than the First, there were still tens of thousands of missing people who had been deported and annihilated in Nazi camps. In 1945, when the prisoners came home and were assembled in front of the Hotel Lutetia in Paris, a nervous crowd of relatives of the missing descended upon the survivors, shouting questions, waving photographs, begging for the slightest information and, especially, any shred of hope.[7] But all hope had been wiped out: the horror of the war was total, and genocide had made it all meaningless. There were those who escaped from the death camps and rebuilt their lives, harboring the guilt of the living who know that others are dead, a survivors' syndrome comparable to what any number of demobilized veterans endured in 1918. The war would last all their lives:[8] "I died in August 1918, on this piece of land; soon it will be thirty-eight years since everything ended for me," wrote Louis Aragon in 1956.[9] But if the experience of war, death, and mourning was overpowering in 1914–1918, collectively as well as individually, it was surely less so in 1939–1945. The testimony of the deportees ran up against society's desire to tune them out and rejoice. This is not to say that the sorrow of the individual in mourning is easier in the context of a collective refusal to suffer. In 2000, the discovery of the last prisoner from the Second World War, an autistic Hungarian locked up for fifty years in a Russian psychiatric hospital, reopened old wounds and rekindled the hopes of the relatives of the missing.[10] Before he was identified by an investigative committee as Andras Thomas, dozens of families claimed him as their brother, uncle, father, or husband; it took only one amazing news item to rekindle the hope of seeing a loved one who had gone missing nearly sixty years earlier. Unlike this Hungarian soldier, who went from complete anonymity to national celebrity, Anthelme Mangin, after arousing the passions of the nation, had been completely forgotten. In the French national memory, apparently there is only room for one unknown soldier.

Notes

INTRODUCTION

1. Paul Bringuier, "La plus poignante histoire de la guerre: l'énigme du soldat inconnu vivant," *L'Intransigeant*, May 11, 1935.
2. Departmental archives, Aveyron, 3X 325. Information given hereafter without reference is from this thick file.

CHAPTER ONE: THE SOLDIER WITHOUT AN ARMISTICE (1918–1922)

1. "Le mystère des poilus inconnus," *Le Courrier de l'Aveyron*, February 5, 1922.
2. "A propos du soldat inconnu," *Le Journal de l'Aveyron*, April 16, 1922.
3. Paul Bringuier, "L'énigme du soldat inconnu vivant," *L'Intransigeant*, May 12, 1935.
4. In *Paris-Soir* and *L'Express du Midi* of January 31, 1935, it was two military policemen who stopped "a man with a blank stare wandering on the quays."
5. Paul Bringuier, "L'énigme du soldat inconnu vivant," *L'Intransigeant*, May 11, 1935; see also "L'inconnu vivant," *Détective*, January 21, 1937.
6. Departmental archives, Rhône, H-Q 729.
7. "Les militaires frappés d'amnésie," *Le Petit Parisien*, January 10, 1920.

8. "Organisation et fonctionnement d'un centre de neuropsychiatrie d'armée," *La Presse médicale*, 1916, p. 78, quoted by Sophie Delaporte in *Le Discours médical sur les blessures et les maladies pendant la Première Guerre mondiale*, history thesis, University of Picardie, 1999, 485 pp., p. 443.

9. For an example of recent attention to these questions, see Louis Crocq, *Les Traumatismes psychiques de guerre* (Paris: Odile Jacob, 1999). See also the third issue of the review *14–18 aujourd'hui*, 2000, about traumatic shock.

10. Sophie Delaporte, op. cit., p. 422.

11. Georges Dumas, *Troubles mentaux et troubles nerveux de guerre* (Paris: Felix Alcan, 1919).

12. A. Porot, A. Hesnard, *Psychiatrie de guerre* (Paris: Felix Alcan, 1919), pp. 17–18, quoted by Frédéric Rousseau, *La Guerre censurée. Une Histoire des combattants européens de 14–18* (Paris: Le Seuil, 1999), 412 pp., pp. 185–86.

13. George L. Mosse, "Le choc traumatique comme mal social," *14–18 aujourd'hui*, 2000, pp. 26–35.

14. This was the point of Dr. André Gilles's research, "Commotionnés et hystériques chez nos ennemis et quelques observations sur la psychologie allemande," *Annales médico-psychologiques*, 1919, quoted by Annette Becker, "Guerre totale et troubles mentaux," *Annales*, January–February 2000, pp. 135–51.

15. As an example, in 1927, Miloch Popovitch proposed in his medical thesis that "war is the primary cause of psychic difficulties." *Sur l'évolution de quelques formes de maladies mentales chez les mobilisés de 14–18*, Bordeaux, 1927, 40 pp., p. 11.

16. A. Fribourg-Blanc, M. Gauthier, *La Pratique psychiatrique dans l'armée* (Paris: Lavauzelle, 1935), 598 pp., p. 138.

17. P. Chavigny, "Psychiatrie aux armées," *Paris Médical*, 1916, quoted by Sophie Delaporte, op. cit., p. 448.

18. Georges Dumas, op. cit.

19. Marc Roudeboush, "Un patient se défend," *14–18 aujourd'hui*, 2000, p. 58.

20. Regarding electrotherapy, see Frédéric Rousseau, "L'électrothérapie des névroses de guerre durant la Première Guerre mondiale," *Guerres mondiales et conflits contemporains* 185 (January 1997), pp. 13–27.

21. For details about this laborious attempt to humanize the war, see Annette Becker, *Oubliés de la Grande Guerre. Humanitaire et culture*

de guerre, populations occupées, déportés civils, prisonniers de guerre (Paris: Noêsis, 1998), 405 pp., pp. 199–228.

22. Ibid., p. 211.
23. Quoted by A. Fenayrou in a letter to the Aveyron prefect, November 25, 1920.
24. Ibid.
25. Medical record opened upon Anthelme Mangin's entry into the Rodez asylum, June 19, 1920.
26. Miloch Popovitch, op. cit., pp. 20–23.
27. Ibid.
28. Ibid., pp. 35–36.
29. Louis Joseph André Régis, *Les Amnésies de guerre. Contribution à l'étude clinique et pathogénique de l'amnésie,* medical thesis, Bordeaux, 1920, 205 pp.
30. Regarding the different characteristics of amnesia, see the study by the psychiatric specialist Georges Génil-Perrin, *Maladies nerveuses et mentales* (Paris: Larousse, 1931), 272 pp., p. 81; and Jean Lépine's chapter on memory problems in *Troubles mentaux de guerre* (Paris: Masson, 1917).
31. Professor E. Régis, "Les troubles psychiques et neuro-psychiques de la guerre," *La Presse médicale,* May 27, 1915; see also "L'amnésie traumatique chez les blessés de guerre," *Le Progrès médical,* June 9 and 16, 1917.
32. Jules Félix Perret, *Contribution à l'étude de l'amnésie simulée,* medical thesis, 1919, Montpellier, 82 pp. In studying delinquents and criminals in the Montpellier region, Betty Grunberg found simulated amnesia in half of her subjects, *Troubles mentaux simulés par les delinquants et les criminels,* medical thesis, Montpellier, 1918.
33. Betty Grunberg, op. cit., p. 78.
34. K. R. Eissler, *Freud sur le front des névroses de guerre* (Paris: Presse Universitaire de France [PUF], 1992), 290 pp., p. 46.
35. Louis Joseph André Régis, op. cit., p. 184.
36. Chantal Beauchamp, *Le Sang et l'imaginaire médical, histoire de la saignée* (Paris: Desclée de Brawver, 2000), 268 pp., p. 82.
37. Louis Joseph André Régis, op. cit., pp. 49–53.
38. "Négativisme amnésique systématique chez un dément," *Revue neurologique,* July–August 1918.
39. Letter from A. Fenayrou to the Aveyron prefect, November 25, 1920.
40. Letter from A. Fenayrou to the prefect, June 23, 1920.

41. The Eure-et-Loir prefect replies negatively to his Aveyron colleague on July 26, 1920.

42. "Les morts vivants. Les cerveaux blessés," *Le Petit Journal,* May 10, 1926.

43. Ibid.

44. These methods are pointed out in *Détective,* January 28, 1937.

45. "Notice concernant un ancien militaire prisonnier de guerre rapatrié d'Allemagne et non identifié," no date or place indicated.

46. In Clermont-Ferrand, Paul Bringuier reported that another amnesiac was identified after having cried out in his sleep with the name of a comrade and his company, in "L'énigme du soldat inconnu vivant," *L'Intransigeant,* May 12, 1935.

47. "Les militaires frappés d'amnésie," *Le Petit Parisien,* January 10, 1920.

48. "Le poilu inconnu de l'asile de Rodez," *Le Matin,* February 24, 1926.

49. "Le poilu inconnu de l'asile de Rodez," *L'Union catholique,* February 25, 1926.

50. Minutes of the Aveyron General Council meeting, May 6, 1926. The French republic is divided into nearly a hundred departments, in each of which the central executive power rests with a prefect, who lives in its capital. For example, the prefect of the department of Aveyron lives in Rodez, its capital. Clermont-Ferrand is the capital of the department of Puy-de-Dôme.

51. Departmental archives, Aveyron, 1 X 250.

52. A. Fenayrou, *Contribution à l'étude des folies rurales. La folie dans l'Aveyron,* medical thesis, Toulouse, 1894.

53. Departmental archives, Aveyron, 1 X 295.

54. This bonus, amounting to 1,500 francs for Fenayrou and 500 francs for his assistant, was given by the Ministry of Pensions.

55. Letter of December 3, 1920, to the prefect.

56. Statement by Mme. Vayssettes, April 19, 1921.

57. Letter from A. Fenayrou to the prefect, September 7, 1920.

58. "Le poilu inconnu de l'asile de Rodez," *Le Matin,* February 24, 1926.

59. Letter from A. Fenayrou to the prefect, January 1, 1929.

60. Letter from Emile Allon to the prefect, November 9, 1920.

61. Letter from A. Fenayrou to the prefect, November 25, 1920.

62. Letter from Emile Allon to the prefect, November 9, 1920.

63. Letter from the prefect to the Rodez police commissioner, December 20, 1920.

64. On August 8, 1921, the supervisor of disputes at the Ministry of Pensions wrote to the Aveyron prefect: "I believe there is no reason to give the so-called Mangin to Mme. Vayssettes."

65. Letter from the prefect to the minister of war, January 21, 1921.

66. Letter from the minister of health to the prefect, March 12, 1921.

67. Letter from the Ministry of Pensions to the prefect, April 16, 1921.

68. Letter from Valentino, August 8, 1921.

69. Martin Le Cann, *Les Aliénés et la loi des pensions militaires*, medical thesis, 1921, Bordeaux, 44 pp.

70. Several articles were devoted to this subject in *La Revue neurologique* in 1916: Dupré, "Réformes, incapacités et gratifications dans les psychoses de guerre," p. 790; J. Lépine, "Réforme et incapacité dans les psychoses," p. 799; Benon, "La guerre et les pensions pour les maladies mentales et nerveuses," p. 320. See also the more general work by Valentino, *L'Indemnisation des infirmités de guerre* (Bordeaux: University Press, 1917).

71. Martin Le Cann, op. cit., p. 29. For details about this law, see Claude Gassiot, *Etude de la loi du 31 mars 1919*, medical thesis, Algiers, 1919; Pierre Souty, *Le Droit à la réparation des invalides de guerre (loi du 31 mars 1919)*, law thesis, Poitiers, 1926, 87 pp.; and Charles Avignon, *La Juridiction des pensions militaires (loi du 31 mars 1919)*, law thesis, Paris: 1944, 148 pp.

72. Report on Anthelme Mangin's situation to the health minister, November 4, 1921.

73. Paul Bringuier, "L'énigme du soldat inconnu vivant," *L'Intransigeant*, May 13, 1935.

74. Deputy from 1898 to 1902, then from 1906 to 1912, and senator from 1912 to 1944. See Jean Joly (dir.). *Dictionnaire des parlementaires français (1889-1940)* (Paris: PUF, 1962).

75. *Journal officiel de la République française*, Senate, 2nd session of December 30, 1921, p. 2489.

76. Ibid.

77. According to this arrangement, on February 1, 1923, Fenayrou sent a bill for 5,565 francs to the Ministry of Pensions for the period from November 28, 1920, to March 31, 1923. Anthelme Mangin's maintenance was estimated at 7 francs a day.

78. *L'Echo national*, quoted by *L'Art funéraire*, February–March 1922, "Il y a six poilus inconnus vivants."

79. "Les six poilus inconnus vivants," *L'Echo national*, January 11, 1922.

80. "Les poilus inconnus vivants. Les trois derniers vont-ils être identifiés?" *La Voix du combattant*, February 5, 1922.

81. *La Voix du combattant*, February 19, 1922.

82. "Les trois inconnus vivants," *Le Matin*, February 19, 1922. During the war, this daily had a circulation of more than 1.6 million. See Stéphane Audoin-Rouzeau, "Bourrage de crâne et information en France en 1914–1918," in Jean-Jacques Becker; Stéphane Audoin-Rouzeau (dir.), *Les Sociétés européennes et la guerre de 1914* (Paris: University of Paris X, 1990), 495 pp.

83. "Pourra-t-on les identifier?" *Le Petit journal*, February 18, 1922.

84. "Le mystérieux aliéné interné à l'asile de Rodez depuis huit ans retrouvera-t-il sa famille?" *Journal des mutilés et combattants*, June 14, 1931.

85. Jean Anouilh, "Vous êtes, comme l'a dit très justement un journaliste de talent, le soldat inconnu vivant," *Le Voyageur sans bagage* (Paris: Gallimard, 1997 [reprint from 1937]), 218 pp., p. 15.

86. "Le mystère des poilus inconnus," *Le Courrier de l'Aveyron*, February 5, 1922.

87. "Les morts vivants," *Le Journal des mutilés et réformés, des anciens combattants et des veuves de guerre*, February 25, 1922.

88. "Les poilus inconnus vivants," *La Voix du combattant*, February 19, 1922.

89. Regarding the myth of fraternity among those in the trenches and an analysis of veterans' patriotism, see Antoine Prost, *Les Anciens Combattants et la société française, 1914–1939* (Paris: Presses de la FNSP, 1977), 3 vol., and in a shorter form, *Les Anciens Combattants* (Paris: Gallimard, 1977), 246 pp.

90. *L'Echo national*, quoted by *L'Art funéraire*, art. cit.

91. As an example, the particular problems of occupied populations and of war prisoners were not taken into account after the war. On the contrary, those in the first category were suspected of Germanization, or associating with the enemy, during the four years' occupation, a suspicion manifested by the myth of the *boche du Nord* ("northern Kraut"), while those in the second category had to fight to obtain the same rights as their comrades who had not known captivity. On this theme of "the forgotten of the Great War," see Annette Becker, op. cit., and Odon Abbal, "Un combat d'après guerre: le statut des prisonniers," *Revue du Nord*, April–June 1998, pp. 405–16.

92. *L'Echo national*, quoted by *L'Art funéraire*, art. cit.

93. "Les poilus inconnus vivants," *La Voix du combattant,* February 19, 1922.
94. "L'inconnu vivant," *Détective,* January 21, 1937.
95. Ibid.

CHAPTER TWO: THE IMPOSSIBLE GRIEF FOR THE MISSING

1. Military losses were estimated at 270 out of 1,000 for 1914, with 240, 199, 105, and 186 out of 1,000 for the following years. See Agnès Fine, Jean-Claude Sangoï, *La Population française au XXe siècle* (Paris: PUF, 1998), 127 pp.
2. Jacques Lecoq, *De la constatation du décès des disparus,* law thesis, Paris, 1921, p. 130.
3. National archives, BB 18 2607 1484-A-18, report to the National Commission on Military Cemeteries, quoted by Yves Pourcher, *Les Jours de guerre* (Paris: Hachette, 1995), 546 pp., p. 469.
4. 2 missing for 1914 and 41 for 1915.
5. 0 missing, 23.8 percent of the total.
6. Pierre Drieu la Rochelle, *La Comédie de Charleroi* (Paris: Gallimard, 1934), 251 pp., p. 32.
7. *Carnets de guerre de Louis Barthas, tonnelier (1914–1918)* (Paris: La Découverte, 1997), 564 pp., p. 184.
8. Paul Truffeau, *1914–1918. Quatre années sur le front* (Paris: Imago, 1998), 244 pp., p. 184.
9. Letter of November 6, 1915, in Jacques Benoist-Méchin, *Ce qui demeure* (Paris: Bartillat, 2000 [reprint]), 273 pp., p. 195.
10. Ibid., p. 196.
11. Thus, soldier Jean-Marie Le Guen wrote his mother on October 7, 1914, to tell her how he had buried his brother, who had been killed in action: "I had a cross made, on one side of which I painted his name, his company, his regiment, and the date of his death, and on the other I engraved his name with a burnt stick. He is buried in a little ravine, about two kilometers north of Perthes, on the right side of the road from Perthes to Tahure. Take note of this information; you will be able to find him if I don't get back there myself, and have his body sent home, so he will be with the family." *Ce qui demeure,* op. cit., p. 70.
12. Henriette de Vismes, *Histoire authentique et touchante des marraines et des filleuls de guerre* (Paris: Perrin, 1918), 298 pp., p. 21.
13. Ibid., p. 119.

14. Departmental archives, Haute-Savoie, 4 M 520.

15. Frédéric Rousseau, *La Guerre censurée,* op. cit., p. 226. The author quotes the instructions from general quarters on June 22, 1916, SHAT 16 N 275.

16. Dominique Richert, *Cahiers d'un survivant. Un soldat dans l'Europe en guerre, 1914–1918* (Strasbourg: La Nuée bleue, 1994), 285 pp., p. 51.

17. "L'identification des soldats tués sur le champ de bataille," *Bulletin de la Société de médecine légale de France,* session of February 8, 1915.

18. Philippe Fougerol, *Décès et disparitions aux armées, constatations et formalités, successions* (Paris: Berger-Levrault, 1915), 63 pp., p. 15.

19. *Bulletin de la Société de médecine légale de France,* session of February 8, 1915.

20. Suzanne Vigneron, *L'Identité des personnes, sa protection légale,* law thesis, Paris, 1937, 183 pp., p. 104.

21. Benjamin Duringer, *La Rectification administrative des actes de décès,* law thesis, Paris, 1920, pp. 51–52.

22. Regarding the history of the expression "*disparition,*" see Sylvie Mouysset, *Apparitions-disparitions,* round table organized in Malves (Aude), May 2000.

23. Jacques Dupâquier, *Histoire de la population française,* vol. 4 (Paris: PUF, 1998), 590 pp., p. 54.

24. *L'Art funéraire et commémoratif,* May 1919 (reprint of an article from *L'Intransigeant* by Lieutenant-Colonel Fabry).

25. "La recherche des disparus," *Le Courrier de l'Aveyron,* April 13, 1922.

26. *Bulletin de l'Union des pères et mères dont les fils sont morts pour la patrie,* April–May–June 1934.

27. "La recherche des corps sur les champs de bataille," *Bulletin de l'Union des pères et mères dont les fils sont morts pour la patrie,* January–June 1939.

28. Ibid.

29. "Mort retrouvé," *L'Ancien Combattant de Paris,* October 10, 1937.

30. The mayor of Mende, Emile Joly, quotes in his journal a notice of someone gone missing that arrived twenty months after the event, in Yves Pourcher, *Les Jours de guerre,* op. cit., p. 307.

31. Stéphane Audoin-Rouzeau, *Cinq deuils de guerre* (Paris: Noêsis, 2001), p. 215.

32. Henriette de Vismes, *Lettres sans réponse* (Paris: Bonne Presse, n.d.), 118 pp.

33. Stéphane Audoin-Rouzeau, *Cinq deuils de guerre,* op. cit., pp. 214–16.

34. Ministère de la Guerre, *Instruction pratique du 2 juin 1916 concernant la constatation aux armées des évacuations, disparitions, décès et inhumations* (Paris: Imprimerie nationale, 1916), 23 pp., p. 14. The annoucement of someone gone missing followed this formula: "We, the undersigned . . . (title of signer of the notice) certify that . . . (first and last names), son of . . .(first and last names of father and mother), born on . . . (date and place of birth, department), serial number . . . , went missing on . . . (date and place of disappearance), and that, since that time, all searches undertaken to find out what happened to him have been futile." The details of the disappearance and presumption of death or of capture followed. Model reprinted by Edgar Trigand-Geneste, *Décès aux armées et dans les hôpitaux à l'Intérieur, disparition. Rôle des maires et des officiers de l'état civil* (Bordeaux: brochure, 1914), 8 pp., p. 5.

35. Yves Pourcher, op. cit., p. 312.

36. Henriette Charasson, *L'Attente, 1914–1917* (Paris: Flammarion, 1929 [1919]), 139 pp., p. 36.

37. This poem, "Les disparus," was often reprinted in the press, notably in *Le Petit Echo en campagne,* October 27, 1918.

38. Correspondence between Jacques and Isabelle Rivière, 1914–1917, quoted by Annette Becker, *Oubliés de la Grande Guerre,* op. cit., p. 164. Alain-Fournier's body was finally found in 1991.

39. Bertha Galeron de Calonne, *Dans la nuit* (Paris: Les Gémeaux, 1925), quoted by Béatrice Bizot, "Une famille de notables pendant la Première Guerre mondiale à travers sa correspondance," master's thesis, Paris IV–Sorbonne, 1990, 140 pp., annexe VIII-b, unpublished.

40. "A une mère," *La Revue hebdomadaire,* December 18, 1915.

41. Letter reprinted by P. d'Estailleur-Chanteraine, *Jacques de Champfeu, gentilhomme, poète et soldat* (Paris: Editions françaises de la Nouvelle Revue nationale, 1922), quoted by Béatrice Bizot, op. cit., annexe VIII-a.

42. *La France de Bordeaux et du Sud-Ouest,* May 11, 1915.

43. Deputy Georges Leredu, member of the civil legislative committee charged with settling judicial problems related to missing persons after the war, recalls, in the preface to the book by Jacques Romanet du Caillaud, several grief-stricken family letters received during the

war, *Les Disparus de la guerre, étude sur la loi du 25 juin, 1919* (Paris: Simon Kra), 133 pp.

44. Yves Pourcher, op. cit., p. 311.

45. "M. Commander of base of the . . . th regiment (office of information for families), I have the honor of informing you that, since . . . , I am without news from my . . . (indicate the relationship), X (first and last names), . . . (rank) in . . . (regiment, batallion, section), . . . (company), serial number . . . , born in . . . on . . . , son of . . . (first and last name of father) and of . . . (first name and maiden name of mother), residing at . . . before mobilization.

"I kindly ask that you communicate to me any information that you might have regarding what happened to this soldier.

"Please accept, M. Commander, the assurance of my respect." In Philippe Fougerol, op. cit., p. 53.

46. Annette Becker, *Oubliés de la Grande Guerre,* op. cit., p. 175.

47. *La Recherche des disparus,* February 28, 1915.

48. *La Recherche des disparus,* December 15, 1917.

49. "Une œuvre de recherche des disparus: Les Nouvelles du soldat," *La Revue hebdomadaire,* December 18, 1915.

50. Francis Latour, *La Papauté et les problèmes de la paix pendant la Première Guerre mondiale* (Paris: L'Harmattan, 1996), 350 pp.

51. Francis Latour, "L'action humanitaire du Saint-Siège pendant la Grande Guerre," *Guerres mondiales et conflits contemporains* 187 (1987), p. 88.

52. Joël Rocafort, *Avant oubli. Soldats et civils de la Côte basque durant la Grande Guerre* (Biarritz: Atlantica, 1997), 699 pp., p. 128.

53. *Bulletin de la Société de médecine légale de France,* session of March 8, 1915.

54. Ibid.

55. *Bulletin des réfugiés du Nord,* September 22, 1915.

56. Rémy Cazals, Claude Marquié, René Pinies, *Années cruelles, 1914–1918* (Villelongue d'Aude: Atelier du gué, 1998), 162 pp., pp. 87–88.

57. "L'amour mutilé," *La Vague,* November 3, 1921.

58. Michel Hanus, "Le travail de deuil," in *Le Deuil,* monograph of the *Revue française de psychanalyse* (Paris: PUF, 1994), 174 pp., pp. 13–32.

59. Sigmund Freud, *Totem et Tabou* (Paris: Gallimard, 1993 [rpt. of *Nouvelle Revue Française,* 1912]), 351 pp.

60. Sigmund Freud, *Considérations actuelles sur la guerre et sur la mort* (1915), in *Essais de psychanalyse* (Paris: Payot, 1998), 274 pp., pp. 7–40.

61. Sigmund Freud, *Deuil et Mélancolie* (1917), in *Métapsychologie* (Paris: Gallimard, 1968).

62. He ends *Considérations actuelles sur la guerre et sur la mort* with this phrase: "Si vis vitam, para mortem. If you want to tolerate life, prepare yourself for death," op. cit., p. 40.

63. Jean Begouin, "La problématique du deuil et le métabolisme de souffrance psychique," in *Le Deuil*, op. cit., pp. 33–50.

64. Yves Pourcher, op. cit., p. 322.

65. Ibid., p. 323.

66. Annette Becker, *La Guerre et la Foi* (Paris: Armand Colin, 1994), 141 pp., pp. 140–41. See also the account of the mourning of the Gallé family, Germaine Francemont's family, in Stéphane Audoin-Rouzeau, *Cinq récits de deuils*, op. cit., pp. 97–141.

67. *La Revue hebdomadaire*, December 18, 1915, art. cit., p. 401.

68. Plaque conserved at the Historial de la Grande Guerre, Péronne, reproduced in Jean-François Sirinelli, Jean-Pierre Rioux, "Le temps des masses," in *Histoire culturelle de la France*, vol. 4 (Paris: Seuil, 1998), 403 pp., p. 127.

69. "Les disparus," *Le Télégramme*, January 29, 1915.

70. *Bulletin de la Société de médecine légale de France*, session of March 8, 1915, art. cit.

71. Ibid.

72. "Nos disparus," *Bulletin des réfugiés du Nord*, August 7, 1915.

73. "Nos ressuscités," *Bulletin des réfugiés du Nord*, August 11, 1915.

74. "A Cam," November 1916, Henriette Charasson, op. cit., p. 58.

75. Ibid., p. 61.

76. Journal de Madeleine Pambrun, October 24, 1918, quoted by Joël Rocafort, op. cit., p. 129.

77. *Bulletin de l'Union des disparus*, March–April 1919.

78. Ibid.

79. *Journal officiel de la République française*, Chambre des députés, session of June 19, 1919.

80. *Bulletin de l'Union des familles de disparus*, May–June 1919.

81. *Bulletin de l'Union des familles de disparus*, July–August 1919.

82. *Journal official de la République française*, Chambre des députés, session of November 11, 1918.

83. *La Dépêche*, November 12, 1918.

84. Annette Becker, "Du 14 juillet 1919 au 11 novembre 1920. Mort, où est ta victoire?," *Vingtième siècle* 49 (January–March 1996), pp. 31–44.

85. *Le Petit Parisien,* July 15, 1919.

86. Patrick Cabanel, *La Question nationale au XIXe siècle* (Paris: La Découverte, 1997), 121 pp., p. 40.

87. Charles Vilain, *Le Soldat inconnu, histoire et culte* (Paris: Maurice d'Hartoy, 1933), 153 pp. Note that unknown soldiers were honored for the first time in the United States after the Civil War. In Cambridge, Massachusetts, a funerary urn carries the following epitaph: "To the unknown dead. A tribute of gratitude to these Union soldiers and sailors of the Civil War 1861–1865, whose resting place is unknown." Ken S. Inglis, "Entombing Unknown Soldiers from London and Paris to Baghdad," *History and Memory* 5 (1993), pp. 7–31.

88. Antoine Prost, *Les Anciens Combattants et la société française,* op. cit., p. 195.

89. "Qui veut être consolé?" *La France de Bordeaux et du Sud-Ouest,* January 5, 1916.

90. Annette Becker lists several gathering places for families of the missing in the Montparnasse, Saint-Ouen, Bagneux, and Ivry cemeteries, *La Guerre et la Foi,* op. cit., p. 109.

91. *Journal officiel de la République française,* Chambre des députés, session of September 12, 1919.

92. Mark Meigs, "La mort et ses enjeux: l'utilisation des corps des soldats américains lors de la Première Guerre mondiale," *Guerres mondiales et conflits contemporains* 175 (July 1994), pp. 135–46.

93. *Le Matin,* November 4, 1920.

94. Quoted by Charles Vilain, op. cit., p. 58.

95. Général Weygand, *Le 11 novembre* (Paris: Flammarion, 1932), 126 pp., p. 91.

96. "Au soldat inconnu du 11 novembre," *L'Univers israélite,* November 26, 1920, quoted by Stéphane Audoin-Rouzeau, Annette Becker, *14–18, Retrouver la guerre,* op. cit., p. 227.

97. *L'Œuvre,* November 13, 1920.

98. Speech by Léon Daudet, *Journal officiel de la République française,* Chambre des députés, session of November 8, 1920.

99. Ibid.

100. Gabriel Boissy, *De Sophocle à Mistral,* 1919, quoted by Olivier Di Scala, *Le Soldat inconnu de l'Arc de triomphe: un symbole d'unité et*

l'éclatement de ces représentations, master's thesis, University of Toulouse-le Mirail, 1999, 143 pp., pp. 20–21.

101. J. A. Durbec, *Gabriel Boissy et le Soldat inconnu,* quoted by Olivier Di Scala, op. cit., pp. 20–21.

102. *Le Matin,* November 4, 1920.

103. *L'Humanité,* November 11, 1920.

104. "Le symbole," *Le Populaire,* November 11, 1920,

105. Stéphane Audoin-Rouzeau, Annette Becker, *14–18, Retrouver la guerre,* op. cit., p. 250.

106. "En passant," *Le Courrier de l'Aveyron,* October 31, 1920.

107. "Un seul poilu inconnu," *La Voix du combattant,* January 2, 1921.

108. See the *Journal des mutilés et réformés* of January 14 and 18, 1922. Finally, a monument to the glory of the North African army was erected on the corniche in Marseille in 1927.

109. Léo Larguier, *Le Soldat inconnu* (Paris: Plon, 1939), 86 pp., pp. 85–86.

CHAPTER THREE: THE RETURN OF COLONEL CHABERT

1. "Qui est l'amnésique inconnu de Rodez?" *Le Journal des mutilés et combattants,* February 3, 1935.

2. *Le Petit journal,* May 10, 1926.

3. Roland Dorgelès, *Les Croix de bois* (Paris: Albin-Michel, 1968 [1919]), 344 pp., p. 342.

4. Jay Winter, *Sites of Memory, Sites of Mourning* (New York: Cambridge University Press, 1995), 310 pp. See the chapter titled "Homecomings: The Return of the Dead," pp. 15–28.

5. "Marié sans l'être," *Le Siècle,* July 4, 1916.

6. *Chez vous, chez moi,* 1918, visa no. 3476, Archives of the Prefecture of Police (A.P.Po) B/A 773. A story in *Le Matin* tells a similar tale, the mistress in this case having not "deserted" but moved out, bringing on the troubles of the escaped soldier, who thinks he has been completely forgotten. "L'infidèle," *Le Matin,* March 2, 1915.

7. *Leur ami,* 1917, visa no. 3160, A.P.Po. B/A 773.

8. Ibid.

9. *Le Retour,* 1918, visa no. 3348, A.P.Po. B/A 773.

10. "Bigamie," *La Française,* July 1, 1916.

11. Charles Le Goffic, *La Guerre qui passe* (Paris: 1918), 383 pp., p. 317.

12. Paul Masson, *Etude sur la bigamie et spécialement dans ses rapports avec le droit civil,* law thesis, Paris, March 9, 1917.

13. Georges Duhamel, *Entretiens dans le tumulte*, from *Récits des temps de guerre*, vol. 2 (Paris: Mercure de France, 1949), 333 pp., p. 95.

14. "Un disparu qui est vivant," *Le Matin*, December 3, 1918.

15. "Furetages," *Le Canard dieppois*, February 15, 1919.

16. There were a few cases of men returning after several years' silence, but those who came back had generally been prisoners of the Ottoman Empire, whose cooperation with international institutions regarding the exchange of prisoner lists was lax. Similarly, Jacques Lecoq speaks in his law thesis about the unhoped-for return in 1920 of a lieutenant from the French military mission in Petrograd, who had been caught up in the revolutionary turmoil and secretly imprisoned in the Peter and Paul Fortress; *De la constatation du décès des disparus*, Paris, 1921, p. 6.

17. "Les veuves pressées," *La Liberté*, August 24, 1916.

18. Jean Caillier, *Les Disparus*, law thesis, Nancy, 1916.

19. Jacques Humblot, *De la conservation par une personne veuve remariée des avantages légaux et conventionnels lui venant de son premier conjoint*, law thesis, Dijon, 1922, p. 9.

20. Ibid., p. 6.

21. Four years' absence were required, ten in cases of proxy (statements by two witnesses affirming a death in cases where no body was found), for the court to order an investigation.

22. Jean Caillier, op. cit., p. 74.

23. Jacques Romanet du Caillaud, *Les Disparus de la guerre*, op. cit., p. vii.

24. Regarding resolution of judicial problems caused by the missing, see Jacques Lecoq, op. cit.

25. "La femme d'un disparu peut-elle se remarier?" *Bulletin des réfugiés du Pas-de-Calais*, March 20, 1919.

26. Regarding this fear of the man who comes back, see Jean-Claude Schmitt, *Les Revenants, les vivants et les morts dans la société médiévale* (Paris: Gallimard, 1994), 306 pp.; and Jean Delumeau, *La Peur en l'occident* (Paris: Hachette, 1993), 607 pp., pp. 103–19.

27. Annette Becker, *La Guerre et la Foi*, op. cit., p. 107.

28. Christiane Amiel, "A corps perdu," *Hésiode* 4 (1994), pp. 27–59.

29. *Journal officiel de la République française*, Chambre des députés, session of June 18, 1915, pp. 921–30.

30. Maurice Barrès authored an offensive article entitled "Le respect des familles," in *L'Echo de Paris*, June 20, 1915.

31. Maurice Barrès, *Scènes et doctrines du nationalisme* (Paris: Plon, 1902), in Raoul Girardet, *Le Nationalisme français, Anthologie 1871–1914* (Paris: Le Seuil, 1983), 275 pp., p. 189.

32. Jacques Péricard, *Face à face: souvenirs et impressions d'un soldat de la Grande Guerre* (Paris: Payot, 1917). For an analysis of this passage from Péricard's book as an anthropological reflection on the body and death, see Leonard V. Smith, "Le corps et la survie d'une identité dans les écrits de guerre français," *Annales,* January–February 2000, pp. 111–33. One finds a similar account of the dead helping the living on the English side of the battle in J. Garnier, *The Visions of Mons and Ypres* (London: R. Banks, 1916), 23 pp.; and Arthur Machen, *The Angels of Mons* (London, 1915), 133 pp.

33. Pierre Drieu la Rochelle, *La Comédie de Charleroi* (Paris: Gallimard, 1934), p. 19.

34. Roland Dorgelès, *Le Réveil des morts* (Paris: Albin Michel, 1949 [1923]), 311 pp., p. 281. The theme of the man who comes back recurs often in Dorgelès, who writes in *Bleu horizon* about missing unburied soldiers who come at night to warm themselves beside the eternal flame on the tomb under the Arc de Triomphe. *Bleu horizon. Pages de la Grande Guerre* (Paris: Albin Michel, 1949), p. 152.

35. "La lanterne des morts," *Journal des mutilés et combattants,* November 10, 1935.

36. "Les morts de la Grande Guerre," *La Femme affranchie,* January 15, 1930.

37. Gigi Damiano, *L'Histoire du Soldat inconnu* (Orléans: Editions de l'en-dehors, 1927), 15 pp., pp. 14–15.

38. Pef, *Zappe la guerre* (Paris: Rue du Monde, 1998).

39. Carine Trévisan, *La Grande Guerre: mort et écriture* (Paris: PUF, 2001), p. 94.

40. William Faulkner, *Monnaie de singe* (Paris: Flammarion, 1987 [*Soldiers' Pay,* New York, 1926], 381 pp.

41. For a succinct analysis of this theme, see R. O. J. Van Nuffel, "Giraudoux, Anouilh, Pirandello et les amnésiques," *Revue générale* 23 (1987), pp. 45–55.

42. Emmanuel Carrère, "L'incroyable histoire du dernier prisonnier de la Seconde Guerre mondiale," *Télérama,* March 21, 2001. See also the program broadcast by "Envoyé spécial" on France 2, on Thursday, March 22, 2001.

43. Abel Moreau, *Le Fou* (Amiens: Edgar Malfère, 1926).

44. Jean Giraudoux, *Siegfried* [four-act play, 1927] (Paris: Le livre de poche, 1991), 476 pp., p. 326.

45. Jean Anouilh, op. cit., pp. 21 and 23.

46. Harald Weinrich, *Léthé. Art et critique de l'oubli* (Paris: Fayard, 1999), 316 pp. See chapter 8, "Le droit à l'oubli, la paix par l'oubli?"

47. Jean Bommart, *Le Revenant* (Paris: A. Lemerre, 1932), 244 pp.

48. Edmond About, *L'Homme à l'oreille cassée* (Paris: Casterman, 1994 [reprinted from 1861 edition]), 212 pp., p. 210.

49. Jean Giraudoux, op. cit., pp. 379–80.

50. Marcel Priollet, *Les Veuves blanches* (Paris: Tallandier, 1926), 254 pp., p. 52.

51. Closer to our time, Sébastien Japrisot takes up the theme of the *Veuves blanches,* leaving out the hatred of Germany and emphasizing the police-procedural side of the investigation. He creates a courageous fiancée, Mathilde, looking for her missing lover, who has become amnesic and has been given to another family after exchanging identities in tragic and fantastic circumstances. *Un long dimanche de fiançailles* (Paris: Gallimard, 1993 [Denoël, 1991]), 373 pp.

52. "L'angoissante énigme," *La Voix des combattants,* May 19, 1928.

53. Leonardo Sciascia, *Le Théâtre de la mémoire* (Paris: Maurice Nadeau, 1984 [Giulio Einaudi, 1981]), 76 pp.

54. *Domenica del corriere,* Sunday supplement of the large daily *Corriere della sera.*

55. On the other hand, it apparently went relatively unnoticed in the French press. See the articles by Henry Bidou in *Le Temps* in September 1931, republished in *Le Petit Marseillais,* September 16 and 17, "Une hallucinante énigme en Italie. Est-ce Bruneri, est-ce Canella?"

56. Luigi Pirandello, *Comme tu veux* (Paris: Gallimard, 1985 [1930]), pp. 607–82.

57. Jorge Luis Borges, "Tom Castro," from *Œuvres complètes* (Paris: Gallimard, 1993), 1,752 pp., pp. 310–15.

58. *La Petite Illustration,* April 10, 1937.

59. Jean Anouilh, *Le Voyageur sans bagage,* op. cit., p. 100.

60. Siegfried, who also wonders about the meaning of his story, a mixture of tragedy and comedy, hears himself answer, "There is a mixture of genres in modern theater." Jean Giraudoux, op. cit., p. 311.

CHAPTER FOUR: THE PILGRIMAGE TO RODEZ

1. "L'inconnu vivant," *Détective,* January 28, 1937; and "L'énigme du soldat inconnu vivant. La confrontation," *L'Intransigeant,* May 14,

1935. On May 10, 1926, *Le Petit Journal* again mentioned two hundred letters received each week by Fenayrou.

2. Out of 292 families, 140 requests concerned a son; 56 a husband; 40 a brother; 29 either a father, a fiancé, a comrade, a cousin, or a nephew; and 27 were not categorized, as they did not mention any relationship.

3. Following the request of Lucien Rivière of la Réunion, Deputy Boussenot came to meet Anthelme Mangin on October 6, 1922. Accompanied by the nephew of the person making the request, he was to bring items (photographs, handwriting sample) for identifying Private Pierre Rivière, missing at Verdun on August 6, 1916.

4. "L'énigme du soldat inconnu vivant," *L'Intransigeant,* May 14, 1935.

5. Correspondence of May 7 and 17 and October 4, 1926, between Fenayrou and the Latvian consulate.

6. Letter from Mme. Lecaille-Wimet, December 9, 1935.

7. Letter from Jeanne Mangin, November 19, 1935.

8. Letter from Mme. Chaillon, February 25, 1926.

9. "Le mystère de l'homme sans nom. Anthelme Mangin est-il Octave-Félicien Monjoin ou Antoine-Marius Gaudin?" *Le Petit Marseillais,* May 25, 1931. Madness following the death of the son is the theme of René Bazin's novel *Baltus le Lorrain* (Paris: Calmann-Lévy, 1926).

10. Letter from Mme. Tugnaire, February 26, 1926.

11. Letter from Mme. Venzac, February 27, 1926.

12. Letter from Mme. Venzac, April 10, 1926.

13. Letter from Mme. Venzac, May 2, 1926.

14. Letter from Mme. Allemersch, April 19, 1926.

15. Letter from Mme. Venzac, May 2, 1926.

16. Letter from Mlle. Reine Grosjean, June 5, 1935.

17. Letter from Mme. Pierson, September 11, 1935.

18. Letter of June 17, 1922. The preceding May 24, accompanied by her son Bonaventure, she had come to Rodez to identify her son Jules, who had been missing since November 1914. Faced with her repeated insistence, Fenayrou, who was skeptical, wrote in his report to the prefect on June 1: "It may seem arrogant to suppose a mother could be mistaken and recognize a man who is a stranger to her as her son. Nevertheless, I couldn't keep from wondering whether Mme. Ceccaldi is not suffering from an illusion."

19. Letter from Mme. Ceccaldi, June 17, 1922.

20. Letter from Victor Rieux, February 4, 1935.

21. Statement of Jean-Baptiste Mazenc, April 23, 1921.

22. Letter from Mme. Pierson, June 18, 1935.

23. Letter from A. Fenayrou to Deputy Boussenot, January 29, 1923.

24. "Les morts vivants," in a poster reprinted by *Le Journal des mutilés*, February 25, 1922.

25. Suzanne Vigneron, *L'Identité des personnes, sa protection légale*, law thesis, Paris, 1937, 183 pp., p. 44.

26. Regarding "bertillonization," see Pierre Darmon, "Bertillon, le fondateur de la police scientifique," *L'Histoire* 105 (November 1987), pp. 42–48.

27. Letter from René Rondot to his parents, November 12, 1914.

28. Letter from Mme. Betton, July 18, 1923.

29. Letter from Mme. Venzac, May 2, 1926.

30. Roger Valade, *La Valeur scientifique de la graphologie*, medical thesis, Lyon, 1921, 71 pp.

31. Edmond Locard, *L'Enquête criminelle et les méthodes scientifiques* (Paris: Flammarion, 1920).

32. Maurice Studer, *Expertise de l'écriture de la main gauche d'après la méthode Locard*, medical thesis, Strasbourg, 1928, 42 pp.

33. Dictations of July 17 and November 21, 1925.

34. Locard does not mention it in his *Mémoires d'un criminologiste* (Paris: Fayard, 1957), 249 pp.

35. "L'énigme du soldat inconnu vivant," *L'Intransigeant*, May 14, 1935.

36. Letter from Mme. Pierson, June 18, 1935.

37. Letter from Jean Dikous, May 11, 1935.

38. Letter from Victor Rieux, February 4, 1935.

39. Letter from Mme. Gastaud-Ivaldi, February 16, 1935.

40. "Le mystère de l'homme sans nom. L'extraordinaire histoire d'un ancien prisonnier de guerre," *Le Petit Marseillais*, May 22, 1931.

41. Fenayrou made this decision following a letter from Mme. Ceccaldi on July 8, 1922. Given the result of the experiment, he did not try again until, on March 30, 1936, M. Fournier asked him to give the patient some clippers, a scythe, or a yoke.

42. "L'énigme du soldat inconnu vivant. La tendresse," *L'Intransigeant*, May 16, 1935. Bringuier described the pitiful experience of a certain Magundo, who succeeded only in putting Mangin completely to sleep.

43. The nephew of François Rogier having gone missing on June 10, 1918, four months after Mangin's discovery, Rogier decided to leave Rodez without meeting the amnesiac on February 21, 1926. Dis-

suaded, Mme. Perraud had already left after the meeting of January 3, 1925, convinced that Mangin was not her son.

44. Letter from the sister of a missing soldier named François Rivière, October 31, 1924.

45. Letter from Mme. Venzac, May 2, 1926.

46. Meeting of August 31, 1922.

47. "La requête et le procès de Mme veuve Henri Mazat," *Le Petit Marseillais,* September 10, 1931.

48. Report of February 28, 1926.

49. Roger Granger said that his brother's legs were hairy and bowed, whereas Mangin's lower limbs were hairless and straight. Finally, a blow-up of a photograph of Fernand Granger showed a prominent vein on his hand, which Anthelme Mangin did not have.

CHAPTER FIVE: AGAINST ALL THE ODDS: THREE ACCOUNTS OF GRIEF

1. Letter from Mme. Delafouilhousse, December 1924.

2. Letter from Mme. Allement, addressed to the president of the Republic, February 12, 1928.

3. "Un disparu de la guerre est reconnu à Rodez," *Le Petit Journal,* April 5, 1922.

4. P. Girard, *De la suppression de la camisole de force dans les asiles d'aliénés,* medical thesis, Montpellier, 1904; J. Manier, *Les Bastilles modernes, mystère des asiles d'aliénés* (Paris: M. Block, 1886), 15 pp.; H. Parrot, *Aperçu critique sur le traitement des maladies mentales dans les asiles publics d'aliénés,* medical thesis, Toulouse, 1900.

5. Albert Londres, *Chez les fous* (Paris: Le serpent à plume, 1997 [Albin Michel, 1925]), 172 pp., p. 169. In 1935, in his medical thesis, Dauzemon also deplores the strange similarity between prison guards and psychiatric nurses, *La Situation du personnel infirmier des asiles d'aliénés* (Paris, 1935), 309 pp.

6. Ibid., p. 155.

7. Anne-Laure Simonot wrote her thesis about Toulouse's work, *Hygiénisme et eugénisme au XXe siècle à travers la psychiatrie française* (Paris: Seli Arsan, 1999), 190 pp.

8. A.D. Aveyron, 1 X 255.

9. "Les déments de la guerre, une mise au point," *Le Courrier de l'Aveyron,* April 9, 1922.

10. "Est-ce une méprise? Le pauvre poilu sera-t-il jamais reconnu par les siens?" *L'Union catholique,* April 10, 1922.

11. "A propos du soldat inconnu," *Journal de l'Aveyron,* April 16, 1922.

12. Letter from Jean Grillon, April 7, 1922.

13. Report from the police prefecture, January 1925.

14. Letter from A. Fenayrou, August 7, 1922.

15. Report from the police prefecture, January 1925, conversation with M. Aubetit, Victor Brille's uncle.

16. Report from A. Fenayrou to the prefect, January 26, 1923.

17. Ibid.

18. Letter from the Brilles, October 18, 1923.

19. Letter from Henry Fougère, March 20, 1923.

20. *Journal officiel de la République française,* Chambre des députés, July 30, 1924, p. 2821.

21. "L'énigme du soldat inconnu vivant. La tendresse," *L'Intransigeant,* May 16, 1935.

22. The Mazats requested the intervention of the king of Spain on February 24, 1917; "L'amnésique de l'asile d'aliénés de Rodez," *La Dépêche,* September 19, 1933.

23. "Vers la fin d'un mystère: l'homme sans nom va-t-il retrouver son identité? La requête et le procès de Mme veuve Henri Mazat," *Le Petit Marseillais,* September 10, 1931.

24. Report from A. Fenayrou to the prefect, June 30, 1922.

25. Letter from Haudeville, July 10, 1922. He wrote again to the ministry on January 17, 1923.

26. Letter from A. Fenayrou to the Aveyron prefect, July 30, 1922.

27. Letter from A. Fenayrou, February 15, 1923.

28. "L'amnésique de l'asile d'aliénés de Rodez," *La Dépêche,* September 12, 1933.

29. "L'amnésique de l'asile d'aliénés de Rodez," *La Dépêche,* September 15, 1933.

30. Letter from A. Fenayrou, August 20, 1924.

31. "Vers la fin d'un mystère: l'homme sans nom va-t-il retrouver son identité? Chez Mme Louise Vayssettes," *Le Petit Marseillais,* September 9, 1931.

32. Request made orally to Fenayrou during a visit with Mangin, August 21, 1923.

33. Letter from Dr. Gouzard, December 15, 1926.

34. Letter from Mme. Mazat, November 12, 1929.

35. Letter from A. Fenayrou, November 29, 1923.

36. "La requête et le procès de Mme veuve Henri Mazat," *Le Petit Marseillais,* September 10, 1931.

37. Carine Trévisan, *La Grande Guerre: mort et ecriture* (Paris: PUF, 2001), p. 95.

38. Letter from Réné Delafoy, November 23, 1922.

39. Letter from A. Fenayrou, December 11, 1922.

40. Ibid.

41. Letter from A. Fenayrou, February 15, 1923.

42. Letter from A. Fenayrou, June 9, 1923, to the minister of health.

43. Letter from A. Fenayrou, January 15, 1923.

44. Letter from the supervisor of disputes at the Ministry of Pensions to the Aveyron prefect, July 20, 1923.

45. Letter from the minister of health, August 4, 1923, to the prefect.

46. Minutes of the general council's deliberations, session of May 6, 1926.

47. Letter from the minister of pensions, July 20, 1923.

48. Letter from Mme. Mangin, January 15, 1925, to the prefect.

49. On January 23, 1927, Mme. Mangin asked the prefect to cancel Mme. Vayssettes's permission to visit.

50. Letter from Mme. Mangin to the Seine prefect, May 20, 1926.

51. Letter from Mme. Mangin, December 27, 1928.

52. Letter from Mme. Mangin to the president of the Rodez court, June 25, 1931.

53. Letter from Mme. Mangin to Deputy Louis Malvy, December 9, 1931.

54. "Un cas curieux," *L'Union catholique,* February 20, 1926.

55. "L'énigme du soldat inconnu vivant. La première mère," *L'Intransigeant,* May 13, 1935.

56. *Le Petit Parisien,* March 2, 1926.

57. On November 9, 1920, when the Ministry of Pensions was considering giving Mangin to Mme. Vayssettes, her honor was questioned in regard to the money she would have come into.

58. Letter from Mme. Mangin, September 30, 1928.

59. Letter from Mme. Mangin, February 21, 1935.

CHAPTER SIX: LEMAY VS. MONJOIN

1. Lucie Lemay's granddaughter's testimony in her memoir, "Grand-mère courage," unpublished manuscript.

2. This letter, furnished by Lucie Lemay as a sample for the handwriting evaluation, is preserved in Anthelme Mangin's file.

3. Military file no. 2039.

4. "L'interné de Rodez, Anthelme Mangin, serait-il Marcel Lemay?" *Le Réveil des combattants,* August–September 1931.

5. "Le retour des grands blessés," *L'Illustration,* August 7, 1915, p. 142.

6. Letter of December 4, 1927, to the minister of pensions, in which Lucie Lemay recognizes her husband, "but so much older."

7. In June 2001, the administration of the International Red Cross (Genève), queried by Lucie Lemay's granddaughter, confirmed what it had said on its card of November 20, 1914.

8. Louise Lemay's memoir, "Grand-mère courage," op. cit.

9. Report of December 23, 1927.

10. Evaluation report from Professor Sorel, May 10, 1928.

11. Report from A. Fenayrou, December 23, 1927.

12. "Le mystère de l'homme sans nom," *Le Petit Marseillais,* May 23, 1931.

13. *L'Intransigeant,* May 15 and 16, 1935.

14. "L'homme qui a retrouvé son nom. La vérité sur le soldat inconnu vivant," *Le Journal magazine,* February 29, 1936.

15. Report of February 18, 1928.

16. Letter from A. Fenayron, February 28, 1928.

17. Evaluation report, May 10, 1928.

18. Ibid.

19. "Pour permettre d'identifier un inconnu vivant de la guerre," *La Voix du combattant,* May 12, 1928.

20. "L'angoissante énigme," *La Voix du combattant,* May 19, 1928.

21. "L'interné de Rodez, Anthelme Mangin, serait-il Marcel Lemay?" *Le Réveil des combattants,* August–September 1931.

22. "L'amnésique de Rodez que vingt familles se disputent retrouvera-t-il enfin les siens?" *Paris-Soir,* January 21, 1935.

23. Report from the asylum director to the prefect, August 31, 1928.

24. "L'interné de Rodez, Anthelme Mangin, serait-il Marcel Lemay?" *Le Réveil des combattants,* August–September 1931.

25. Letter from A. Fenayrou to the prefect, October 2, 1928.

26. Letter from Foucault published in *Le Réveil des combattants,* August–September 1931.

27. "A Saint-Maur-sur-Indre avec la famille Monjoin," *Le Petit Marseillais,* September 14, 1931.

28. Speech of the mayor of Saint-Maur-sur-Indre, Anselme Patureau-Mirand, at the tomb of Octave Monjoin, in *Centre-Eclair*, April 5, 1948: "Thanks to the devotion and generosity of men of goodwill, the body of Octave Monjoin, the Rodez amnesiac, lies henceforth in his native soil."

29. *Centre-Eclair*, March 23, 1948.

30. Letter of May 13, 1930, in Anthelme Mangin's file.

31. "A Saint-Maur-sur-Indre avec la famille Monjoin," *Le Petit Marseillais*, September 14, 1931.

32. Ibid.

33. "Le professeur Sorel conclut que l'amnésique Anthelme Mangin doit s'appeler en réalité Octave Félicien Monjoin," *Le Petit Marseillais*, September 13, 1931.

34. Letter from A. Fenayrou, November 30, 1930, to the Aveyron prefect.

35. Letter from the Aveyron prefect, December 5, 1930.

36. Letter from the Ministry of Pensions to the Aveyron prefect, March 7, 1931.

37. "A Saint-Maur-sur-Indre avec la famille Monjoin," *Le Petit Marseillais*, September 14, 1931.

38. Report from the prefect to the minister, April 4, 1931.

39. "Un ancien prisonner du camp de Hameln confirme que l'interné de Rodez est bien Octave Félicien Monjoin," *Le Petit Marseillais*, September 22, 1931. The article was reprinted in particular in *Le Courrier de l'Aveyron* and *L'Union catholique*, October 4 and 8, respectively.

40. Report furnished by the German authorities and presented at the Rodez trial, November 1937.

41. For example, "Qui est le soldat no. 13 interné à l'asile de Rodez?" *L'Echo de Paris*, May 27, 1931.

42. "Le soldat inconnu mais vivant à l'asile d'aliénés de Rodez," *La Croix*, May 30, 1931.

43. "L'interné de Rodez serait-il Marcel Lemay? Une pénible et douloureuse affaire!" *Le Réveil des combattants*, August–September 1931.

44. Ibid.

45. "Le soldat inconnu mais vivant à l'asile d'aliénés de Rodez," *La Croix*, May 30, 1931.

46. "Pour améliorer le sort des aliénés de la guerre," *Journal des mutilés et combattants*, March 14, 1932.

47. Letter from the Ministry of Pensions, June 15, 1933, to the prefect.
48. "L'aliéné de Rodez sera-t-il enfin identifié?" *Le Progrès de l'Indre,* March 11, 1933.
49. "L'amnésique de Rodez que se disputent vingt familles retrouvera-t-il enfin les siens?" *Paris-Soir,* January 21, 1934.
50. "Un homme va retrouver son nom. Devant le tribunal de Rodez, l'amnésique Anthelme Mangin est revendiqué par six familles. Mais il apparaît que Mangin est bien Octave Monjoin de Saint-Maur." *Le Progrès de l'Indre,* February 2, 1935.
51. "Le soldat sans nom," *Le Courrier de l'Aveyron,* October 1, 1933.
52. "On avait retrouvé le passé de l'homme sans nom," *Match,* April 13, 1939.
53. "L'amnésique de Rodez," *La Dépêche,* November 16, 1933.
54. This message was published in *Le Courrier de l'Aveyron* on October 15, 1933.
55. "Les décisions," *L'Intransigeant,* May 19, 1935.
56. This information from sources close to Lucie Lemay was used by Yves Gaël in *Le Journal magazine* of February 21, 1936, the *Journal des mutilés et combattants* of November 19, 1933, and *Le Courrier de l'Aveyron,* October 15, 1933.
57. *Journal des mutilés et combattants,* November 29, 1933, "On se dispute toujours Anthelme Mangin, l'amnésique de Rodez."

CHAPTER SEVEN: THE DOUBLE DEATH OF ANTHELME MANGIN

1. The file was lost somewhere between the departmental archives of Aveyron, Montpellier, and the supreme court; my attempts to locate it have been fruitless.
2. Letter from the Indre prefect to his counterpart in Aveyron, December 5, 1933.
3. Departmental archives, Aveyron, minutes of verdicts, Rodez court, March 6, 1935.
4. "L'énigme du soldat inconnu vivant. Les décisions," *L'Intransigeant,* May 19, 1935.
5. Georges Viriot, *Considérations sur l'abcès de fixation,* medical thesis, Paris, 1926, 80 pp.
6. *Bulletin de la Société de médecine des hôpitaux de Paris:* session of April 30, 1926.

7. No report about this operation was preserved in Anthelme Mangin's file. This information was in a letter from the prosecutor of the Republic to the Aveyron prefect, June 14, 1935.

8. "L'affaire de l'aliéné inconnu devant le tribunal civil de Rodez," *L'Union catholique,* January 31, 1935; "Le sort du soldat inconnu de Rodez," *Le Courrier de l'Aveyron,* February 10, 1935; "Le procès sensationnel de l'amnésique inconnu," *La Petite Gironde,* January 31, 1935; "Un curieux procès," *Le Mémorial des Deux-Sèvres,* February 3, 1935.

9. Regarding the refutation of Dr. Andrée Deschamps's experiment, see "Le procès de l'aliéné inconnu," *L'Union catholique,* January 30, 1935.

10. "Le soldat vivant inconnu de Rodez," *La Petite Gironde,* February 4, 1935.

11. Monjoin, Lemay, and Mazat.

12. *Le Matin,* January 31, 1935.

13. "Qui est l'amnésique inconnu de Rodez?" *Journal de mutilés et combattants,* February 3, 1935.

14. "Vers la reconnaissance de l'amnésique Anthelme Mangin," *La Voix du combattant,* February 9, 1935.

15. "Qui est le mystérieux Anthelme Mangin?" *La Dépêche,* January 31, 1935.

16. Letter from the minister of pensions, January 31, 1935.

17. Letter from the prosecutor of the Republic to the prefect, June 14, 1935.

18. Letter from Deschamps to the ministers of public health and pensions, and to the Aveyron prefect, June 17, 1935.

19. Departmental archives, Aveyron, minutes of the verdict of the Rodez court, March 6, 1935.

20. "L'affaire Anthelme Mangin ou l'aliéné inconnu," *L'Union catholique,* March 7, 1935.

21. "L'aliéné inconnu a quitté l'asile de Rodez," *Le Courrier de l'Aveyron,* March 29, 1936.

22. The Perray-Vaucluse Hospital, Anthelme Mangin's administration file.

23. In March, 1937, Dr. Génil-Perrin justified this decision thus: "We had to completely isolate the patient, to remove him from influences that were bound to be there. It was to create an atmosphere of calm

and tranquility for him that, in spite of ourselves, we had to resist all the efforts many people made to approach him." "L'amnésique de Rodez," *Le Socialiste aveyronnais,* March 20, 1937.

24. Ibid.

25. "L'amnésique de Rodez va-t-il être enfin identifié? Des cicatrices l'ont fait reconnaître des habitants d'un village de Savoie," *La Petite Gironde,* March 19, 1936.

26. "L'amnésique de Rodez est-il un habitant de la Corrèze?" *L'Union catholique,* March 10, 1937.

27. "L'homme qui a retrouvé son nom. La vérité sur le soldat inconnu vivant," *Le Journal magazine,* February 29, 1936.

28. "Le soldat inconnu vivant va-t-il enfin avoir un nom?" *Journal des mutilés et combattants,* January 17, 1937.

29. "L'amnésique de Rodez," *Le Socialiste aveyronnais,* March 20, 1937.

30. "Confrontation dramatique de l'inconnu vivant de Rodez avec les familles qui le revendiquent," *Le Matin,* January 13, 1937.

31. "Pour donner une famille à l'amnésique de Rodez," *La Voix du combattant,* January 16, 1937.

32. "Confrontation dramatique de l'inconnu vivant de Rodez avec les familles qui le revendiquent," *Le Matin,* January 13, 1937; "Encore l'amnésique de Rodez," *L'Union catholique,* January 14, 1937.

33. "'C'est mon fils! Il faut qu'on me le rende' déclare avec conviction Mme Mangin de Nantes, qui entend le ramener dans sa ville natale," *L'Intransigeant,* January 19, 1937; "L'amnésique de Rodez," *La Petite Gironde,* January 19, 1937.

34. "Un bien curieux procès," *L'Excelsior,* January 12, 1937. The article was reprinted in *Le Mémorial des Deux-Sèvres,* January 14, 1937, and in "Le soldat inconnu vivant va-t-il surgir de la nuit où depuis vingt ans il est enseveli? Rendra-t-on à Madame Lemay l'époux qu'elle n'a pas désespéré de retrouver?" *Le Journal,* January 30, 1937.

35. *L'Excelsior,* January 12, 1937.

36. Departmental archives, Rhône, H-Q 729.

37. "Anthelme Mangin, l'amnésique de Rodez, va reprendre avant peu son véritable nom," *Le Progrès de l'Indre,* January 16, 1937.

38. "Un coup de théâtre! Une lettre prouverait que le soldat inconnu vivant n'a jamais été un inconnu. Il s'appellerait Octave Monjoin," *L'Excelsior,* January 14, 1937.

39. "L'amnésique de Rodez est toujours réclamé par deux familles qui attendent avec impatience la sentence que les experts rendront dans un mois," *La Petite Gironde,* January 15, 1937.

40. "L'amnésique de Rodez est officiellement identifié par les experts médicaux," *La Petite Gironde*, March 13, 1937; "Le soldat inconnu de Rodez," *Le Courrier de l'Aveyron*, March 14, 1937; "L'amnésique de Rodez," *Le Mémorial des Deux-Sèvres*, March 13, 1937.

41. "Anthelme Mangin l'amnésique de Rodez va reprendre avant peu son véritable nom," *Le Progrès de l'Indre*, January 16, 1937.

42. "Du drame au vaudeville ou . . . attendra-t-on que Mangin soit mort pour lui redonner son nom?" *Le Progrès de l'Indre*, April 10, 1937.

43. "L'affaire Monjoin approche de sa conclusion," *Le Progrès de l'Indre*, May 29, 1937.

44. Article 118 of the April 16, 1930, finance law allows the descendants of the insane interned during war to receive the same pension as that given to the interned soldier's wife. "L'après-guerre, bulletin de la fédération départementale aveyronnaise des anciens combattants," August 1931, "Pour les ascendants d'aliénés."

45. This request was made by the Monjoins on November 8, 1933, via the intermediary of the Indre prefect, who wrote to his counterpart in Aveyron.

46. "Le soldat inconnu vivant aura bientôt un nom. Ce que dit le docteur Génil-Perrin, l'un des trois experts chargés d'examiner l'amnésique de Rodez," *L'Ancien Combattant de Paris*, March 21, 1937.

47. "Le soldat inconnu vivant va-t-il enfin recouvrer son état civil? Il est maintenant hors de doute qu'il s'agit d'Octave Monjoin," *L'Ancien Combattant de Paris*, April 11, 1937.

48. Departmental archives, Aveyron, minutes of the verdict of the Rodez court, November 16, 1937.

49. Ibid.

50. "Le tribunal de Rodez décide que l'amnésique Anthelme Mangin est bien Octave Monjoin de Saint-Maur," *Le Progrès de l'Indre*, November 20, 1937.

51. "Le soldat inconnu vivant a retrouvé son nom," *L'Ancien combattant de Paris*, November 21, 1937.

52. "L'Affaire de l'amnésique de Rodez. Le jugement du tribunal de Rodez identifie Monjoin," *L'Union catholique*, November 17, 1937.

53. For an account of the January 12 hearing, "Encore l'amnésique de Rodez," *Le Courrier de l'Aveyron*, January 22, 1939.

54. Departmental archives, Hérault, minutes taken by the Montpellier court of appeals clerk, March 8, 1939.

55. "L'amnésique de Rodez devient officiellement Octave Monjoin," *Journal des mutilés et combattants,* March 12, 1939.

56. "La cour d'appel de Montpellier s'est prononcée: l'amnésique de Rodez est Octave Félicien Monjoin de Saint-Maur," *Le Progrès de l'Indre,* March 11, 1939.

57. The peasant expression in the original text, "to do one's twenty-eight days," means to die.

58. *Le Progrès de l'Indre,* March 11, 1939.

59. "Nous apprenons aujourd'hui que, par l'entremise de M. David, avocat à Niort, son défenseur, [madame Lemay] vient de signer un pourvoi en cassation contre l'arrêt de la cour de Montpellier," "L'affaire de l'amnésique de Rodez," *Le Mémorial des Deux-Sèvres,* March 12, 1939.

60. Saint-Maur-sur-Indre municipal archives, death certificate.

61. "L'amnésique de Rodez est plus seul que jamais," *Le Courrier de l'Aveyron,* April 9, 1939.

62. "On avait retrouvé le passé de l'homme sans nom," *Match,* April 13, 1939.

63. "L'amnésique de Rodez est plus seul que jamais," *Le Courrier de l'Aveyron,* April 9, 1939.

64. In the absence of historical studies, the primary reference work on this subject, despite its controversial nature, remains that of the expert Max Lafont, *L'Extermination douce. La mort de 40,000 malades mentaux dans les hôpitaux psychiatriques en France sous le régime de Vichy* (Paris: Editions de L'AREFPI, 1987), 255 pp.

65. Paul Weindling, *L'Hygiène de la race. Hygiène raciale et eugénisme médical en Allemagne* (Paris: La Découverte, 1998), 301 pp. For the French case, see Anne Carol, *Histoire de l'eugénisme en France* (Paris: Le Seuil, 1995), 373 pp.

66. Max Lafont, op. cit., pp. 56, 59.

67. "Le mystère de l'homme sans nom. L'extraordinaire histoire d'un ancien prisonnier de guerre," *Le Petit Marseillais,* May 22, 1931.

68. "September tenth, nineteen hundred forty two, seven thirty A.M., Octave Félicien Monjoin died, 1 rue Cabanis, no known domicile, born in Saint-Maur (Indre), March 19, eighteen hundred ninety one, profession unknown, unmarried," death certificate, Paris municipal archives, 14 arrondissement city hall.

69. "Revendiqué par 100 000 familles, Octave Monjoin, la plus inhumaine épave de la Grande Guerre repose aujourd'hui dans un coin de terre anonyme," *Actu,* March 12, 1944.

70. Letter reprinted by Joël Moreau in *Un peu d'histoire de Saint-Maur-sur-Indre* (s.l., n.d.), 103 pp., chapter about Mangin, pp. 88–96. The italics indicate Marcel Boucton's underlinings.

71. Saint-Maur-sur-Indre municipal archives, minutes of the municipal council deliberations.

72. Louise Lemay, "Grand-mère courage," op. cit.

73. The account of these three days is reconstructed here based on regional press, to wit: *Centre-Éclair,* April 5, 1948; *La Nouvelle république du Centre-Ouest,* April 5, 1948; *La Marseillaise (Berry-Tourraine-Marche),* April 5, 1948; *L'Emancipateur de l'Indre,* April 10–17, 1948.

CONCLUSION

1. "Grâce au dévouement et à la générosité d'hommes de coeur: le corps d'Octave Monjoin, l'amnésique de Rodez, repose désormais dans sa terre natale." *Centre-Éclair,* April 5, 1948.

2. Jean Giraudoux, *Siegfried et le Limousin,* (Paris: Le livre de poche, 1991), p. 291.

3. "Vers la fin d'un mystère: l'homme sans nom va-t-il retrouver son identité?" *Le Petit Marseillais,* September 8, 1931.

4. *Journal de l'Aveyron,* April 16, 1922.

5. *L'Union catholique,* March 7, 1935.

6. *Détective,* January 21, 1937.

7. Annette Wieviorka, *Déportation et genocide. Entre la mémoire et l'oubli* (Paris: Hachette, 1995 [Plon, 1992]), 506 pp., pp. 86–87.

8. Regarding Survivors' Syndrome, see Anny Dayan-Rosenman, "Survivants de la Shoah: la parole de Lazare," *Les Temps modernes,* 2001; Jay Lifton, *Death in Life, Survivors of Hiroshima* (New York: Vintage Books, 1969).

9. Louis Aragon, *Le Roman inachevé,* quoted by Carine Trévisan, *La Grande Guerre: mort et ecriture* (Paris: PUF, 2001), p. 130.

10. Regarding the story of this Hungarian soldier, see the program on France 2, *Envoyé special,* broadcast Thursday, March 22, 2001, and the account of Emmanuel Carrère in *Télérama,* March 21, 2001, "56 ans dans un asile russe," pp. 10–22.

About the Author

JEAN-YVES LE NAOUR teaches history and political science at the University of Aix-en-Provence, France. His previous titles include *A History of Sexual Behavior during World War I*. *The Living Unknown Soldier* will be published in six languages.